Mr. Augustus John Roe, himself a dedicated, learned, and accomplished martial artist in his own right, offers this tribute to martial arts heroes and partakers of their legacies. For the martial artist, his straightforward retellings of the lives of obscure figures such as the Vietnamese swordswoman Bùi Thị Xuân and Thai pugilist Nai Khanom Tom, alongside more popular martial celebrities like Musashi and Bruce Lee, place these personalities' exploits in comparative context, which allows the reader to explore the nuances and diversity of martial arts storytelling—all the while intimating divergent prospective paths for the aspiring martial artist.

Furthermore, Mr. Roe's Legend-Facts-Functions structure makes the book especially suitable for the classroom as a sourcebook for storytelling that compels the learner to question the nature and meaning of history and mythmaking as well as investigate their own presumptions about the value of a good story.

> — Quảng Huyền PhD, Dharma
> Master, senior lecturer of
> Vietnamese history and culture

This book approaches a very interesting area of martial arts. Within the lives of these legends, we seem to find the same ascetic practices in one form or another, all constituted by training that helps each to reach a very high level of skills in their art or attainment of enlightenment.

With good style, the author depicts the stories of different masters, through different times and places in history. A must-read for any martial arts practitioner wanting to learn more about legendary masters from the past.

> — Clement Martin, Head Instructor
> Kishinkai Vietnam

This book examines various martial arts legends through the lens of four thematic topics as to their factuality and the lessons and value that could be derived from them for martial arts practitioners.

I especially enjoyed the segment about Bùi Thị Xuân in the Challenges section. The question arose in my mind as to whether her legend otherwise motivated the women fighters in the Viet Cong and Viet Minh. It is not common today to see women as frontline fighters beyond support roles, excepting possibly the Kurd YPJ. Bùi Thị Xuân was an early role model for women's liberation and reflected that woman do not need men to protect them.

I would certainly recommend this book to those interested in the lessons derived from these legendary masters of martial arts.

In my own case, the book's framework is now helping me with an ongoing examination of the legends and myths of a particular Asian martial art. I expect other readers may find this framework useful in their own examination of a martial art system.

> — Moe Gyo, fifty-year practitioner
> of Japanese and Southeast Asian
> Martial Arts, Krav Maga

Augustus John Roe dissects important figures from the world of martial arts, where legends and history often merge. Once again, he offers us a rich contribution to the field of Martial Arts Studies.

> — Mickael Langlois, Ph.D., author,
> martial arts researcher

LEGENDARY MASTERS OF THE MARTIAL ARTS

LEGENDARY MASTERS OF THE MARTIAL ARTS

Unraveling Fact from Fiction

Augustus John Roe

YMAA Publication Center
Wolfeboro, NH USA

YMAA Publication Center, Inc.
PO Box 480
Wolfeboro, NH 03894
800-669-8892 • www.ymaa.com • info@ymaa.com

ISBN 9781594399626 (print)
ISBN 9781594399633 (ebook)
ISBN 9781594399640 (hardcover)

Cover design by Axie Breen
Photos provided by the authors unless otherwise indicated.
Edited by Doran Hunter
This book typeset in Palatino and Cochin

20230817

Publisher's Cataloging in Publication

Names: Roe, Augustus John, 1988- author.

Title: Legendary masters of the martial arts : unraveling fact from fiction / Augustus John Roe.

Description: Wolfeboro, NH USA : YMAA Publication Center, [2023] | Includes bibliographical references.

Identifiers: ISBN: 9781594399626 (softcover) | 9781594399640 (hardcover) | 9781594399633 (ebook) | LCCN: 2023942875

Subjects: LCSH: Martial artists--Biography. | Martial artists--Legends. | Martial arts--History. | Martial arts--Biography. | Southeast Asia--History. | Southeast Asia--Legends. | BISAC: SPORTS & RECREATION / Martial Arts / General. | HISTORY / Asia / Southeast Asia. | SOCIAL SCIENCE / Folklore & Mythology.

Classification: LCC: GV1113.A2 R64 2023 | DDC: 796.8092--dc23

Printed in USA.

CONTENTS

INTRODUCTION

Martial arts transport us to the realms of legends. Every single day, countless stories are told of history's martial heroes: warriors that overcame seemingly impossible odds to defeat their enemies, find spiritual transcendence, or simply survive.

Whether these tales appear orally from student-to-student, on the big or small screen, or in the form of the written word, they remain a key element of martial culture.

Although the legends of historical martial arts warriors are undoubtedly gripping, playing on our darkest fears and tugging at our heartstrings with acts of hope, adversity, and triumphs of the human spirit, they often cause one to wonder where fact ends and fiction begins.

No stories are more gripping than those surrounding the founders and great masters of modern-day practices. It is with these legendary figures and their tales that this book concerns itself.

The "hero" and "underdog" story structures, a staple of humanity since antiquity, are commonplace throughout the canon of martial arts legends, with their familiar plot points and character types. For example, the student being frail or sickly, their study being prohibited by parents or other authority characters, an (often old) mentor figure teaching them ancient secrets, and a final test of skills that must be undertaken alone.

The protagonists of each martial arts legend are varied, and may be of different genders, ages, or backgrounds. They may face a spiritual crisis, a physical enemy, a natural enemy, or even be their own greatest enemy.

However, it cannot be ignored that we *do* often see specific formats and themes reoccurring in supposedly real-life events. This then raises the question: "Do we tell the legends of martial arts figures because of their magnificent characters and gripping stories, or do we insert these elements into what may be far more mundane realities?"

This is a conundrum that this book intends to investigate further by examining three key questions.

- Why are the legendary martial arts founders and figureheads held in such high regard?
- How factual are their legends?
- What is the function of these legends, both historically and in the modern day?

Twelve "true" tales of some of the most legendary martial arts figures will be presented in this book. These legends have been specifically selected as they represent a spread of well-known martial arts communities (rather than just a single style or nation), and because they are highly dramatic and widespread in numerous formats.

The following legends have been divided into four thematic categories, based upon what is widely considered to be their key content (however, these categories are subject to personal interpretation, as many of the tales could be placed into two or more).

These categories include:

1. Spiritual Journeys
2. Rebellion Tales
3. Duels
4. Challenges

The legends will first be retold as they commonly appear within informal martial arts histories, usually repeated orally, seen in film or television, or other media formats. We will then examine the known facts about each figure and legend, present possible reasons for their longevity, and discuss key functions that they have served for followers and practitioners of martial arts both historically and in the modern world.

In the final part of the book, we will examine common themes and motifs throughout these legends and return once again to ruminate upon their functions.

NOTES ON WRITING

Although the terms "myths" and "legends" are often used interchangeably, they can be distinguished by two key differences.

Myths are traditional stories that often incorporate aspects of the supernatural and may be entirely fictional. In contrast, legends are typically based upon verifiable historical characters. Second, while often incredible, legends rarely cross into the realm of what is clearly impossible. It is with these legends that this book concerns itself.

Regarding the content, the martial arts being examined here are "traditional" Eastern martial arts. These are usually Asian-developed systems that incorporate the use of forms/ kata and focus on the spiritual and mental aspects of training alongside the physical, rather than pure combat sports.

It is also important to highlight that focusing upon the facts of these legends is not an attempted "debunking" or "defamation" of martial arts masters and figureheads. Instead, each legend will be presented alongside the known facts (or lack thereof). Therefore, it is up to the reader to draw their own conclusions about the content discussed.

For the most part, all names and foreign language words have been romanized following standard conventions.

For words written in English with diacritical markings and romanizations of Chinese/Japanese/other languages, I have used italics for the first appearance to highlight that it is a foreign language. From that point onwards, I have used standard American English without accents, tones, or italics.

The legends told at the beginning of each section have intentionally been left uncited except for dialogue. This is a deliberate exclusion, as these tales are typically not dependent on reliable sources and are often shared orally within martial arts communities, or dramatized in film, media, and written interpretations. Therefore, they seldom have a fixed original source or form.

Dialogue used within the legends is based on records of conversations or writings from the figures and has been cited in the references. However, in some cases this speech has not been written verbatim and may have been adapted slightly to better fit the narrative.

At the start of each legend, you will find an overview of each main figure of the story. This includes basic aspects such as their life and death dates, but also examples of what they are known for and why, as well as notes surrounding the figure(s) that are pertinent to the legend.

Part I

SPIRITUAL JOURNEYS

This section will look at three legendary figures of martial arts who are widely known for their spiritual legacies in Buddhism, Taoism, and Shintoism, respectively. These are Bodhidharma, Zhang Sanfeng, and Morihei Ueshiba.

While the legends of these figures take place many centuries apart, they all detail journeys undertaken that focus on spiritual and religious awakenings, either for the figures themselves or their followers.

Similarly, they have been categorized this way due to the key aspects of their legends historically, and the relevance they hold in the modern world. In this respect, we know each of the three figures for their contributions to the religious and spiritual sides of martial arts as much as for their physical contributions.

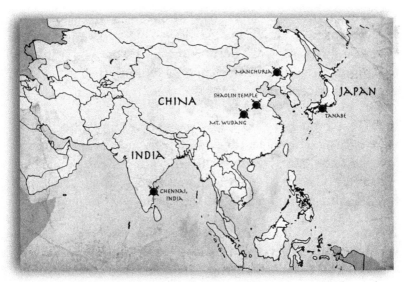

Key sites from Chapter One: Chennai (India), Mount Wudang, the Shaolin Temple, and Manchuria (China), and Tanabe (Japan).

BODHIDHARMA
A Zen Monk's Journey to the East

Bodhidharma was born as *Bodhitāra*. He is known as Daruma in Japanese and Da Mo in Chinese. Bodhidharma is reported to have been born as the third son of a southern Indian king (possibly in the Chennai region) during the fifth or early sixth century.

If so, he would have been raised as an elite member of the warrior caste. This means he would likely have been trained in unarmed combat, wrestling, stick-fighting, swordsmanship, and military strategy. He also may have studied yogic and Buddhist breathing and flexibility exercises.

The dates of Bodhidharma's death are disputed, and some versions of his story claim that he lived until one-hundred-fifty or even older. Meanwhile, folktales from the era often recount him appearing in the region long after his alleged death.

Bodhidharma is often portrayed in paintings and stories with dark skin and thick black hair. Some texts, however, portray him as having blue eyes and a lighter complexion and claim he was of Persian descent. Bodhidharma is usually pictured with a large beard, earrings, and dark brown or orange robes of the Buddhist clergy. In most modern depictions, he wears a twisted expression, displaying either sternness or anger.

He is known today as the founder of Zen (Chan) in China, an introspective school of Buddhism that believes the truth lies within oneself rather than in external sources. He is also known as the Patriarch Master of the Shaolin Temple, Chinese Kung Fu, and by extension, many schools of Asian martial arts.

Legends of Bodhidharma appear in many countries throughout Asia. He is seen as a forefather of martial arts by many groups that have been influenced by Chinese culture over the centuries, including Japan, Korea, Vietnam, and the nations of the Malay Archipelago.

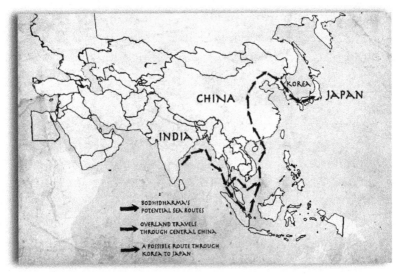

Possible routes of Bodhidharma's journey to East Asia.

The Legend

For more than two years, Bodhidharma traveled on nothing more than his own two feet, dedicated to fulfilling his dying master's ultimate wish. His goal was to spread the word of Zen in the great kingdom beyond the mountains.

Many monks had ventured east before Bodhidharma, though very few had ever returned, and those that did told of a bizarre land, cold and hard, divided by war and rife with suffering. It seemed the task he had been presented with would prove impossible.

At first, he trekked across the wetlands and grassy plains of western India before facing the vast mountain ranges that lay to the east. Over the next year, Bodhidharma weaved a path through the wild Himalayan lowlands before eventually emerging into Southeast Asia. The last leg of the Zen monk's epic journey was by boat. He set foot in southern China for the first time in the year 527 CE. Keen to make headway on his challenge at last, Bodhidharma ventured to the city of Jian Kang, the seat of Imperial power. Supposedly, Emperor Wu, the leader of the Liang Dynasty, was an avid follower of Buddhism. If he could bring the message of Zen to the nation's ruler, then maybe Bodhidharma's mission would have a chance of success.

As he approached the city walls, an escort of guards met the monk. It seemed word of his quest had already reached the city, and the opportunity to meet a wandering holy man from the lands of the Buddha himself was a tempting offer for the pious emperor.

The soldiers escorted Bodhidharma through the streets of a bizarre and foreign city, filled with thousands of people, sights, sounds, and smells that were alien to the monk. Eventually, they reached the gates of the Imperial Palace and led the monk through into a lavish great hall where the emperor was seated drinking tea.

Bodhidharma bowed low, to which Wu responded with a friendly nod. The meeting had started well. Bodhidharma had studied the local language while traveling, and this impressed Emperor Wu. The emperor was intrigued by the monk's mysterious nature and soon questioned him on the nature of Zen Buddhism.

"What do you think is the highest meaning of the noble truth?"

"There is no noble truth," Bodhidharma replied.

The emperor stroked his beard in thought. "Well then, how much karmic merit do you think I have accumulated from my work? I have built vast temples, ordained hundreds of monks, and copied tens of thousands of sutras."

The monk took a breath. He was never one to skirt around the truth. "I believe you have accumulated none."[1]

As respectfully as possible, Bodhidharma explained how, in the pursuit of true enlightenment, one must journey inward rather than outward.

Emperor Wu took offense to the claim that all of his devotion had achieved nothing and expelled Bodhidharma from his city.

The monk was stunned that the meeting that had seemed so promising just a short time before had ended in abject failure. Bodhidharma swallowed his pride, deciding this was Karma and that his faith must not wane in the face of hardship.

* * *

Making his way deeper into the vast country, Bodhidharma soon found himself staring upward at the peak of Mount Song. It was one of China's five sacred Taoist sites and home to one of the emperor's most important Buddhist monasteries. Maybe speaking with the monks themselves would prove more fruitful than it had been with their ruler.

Unfortunately, word had already reached the abbot that a bizarre-looking, huge, hairy man with dark skin and blue eyes was traveling through their lands, spreading a false message of Buddhism.

The abbot called out through the gates on seeing the stranger approach the temple, declaring that he was unwelcome. Respectfully, as always, Bodhidharma bowed his head and thanked the abbot for his time.

Never one to be easily disheartened, the Zen monk decided to meditate on his dilemma. Finding a cave on the northern side of the mountain, Bodhidharma took the weight off his aching feet and sat cross-legged with his eyes fixed upon the wall in a distant stare.

As he gazed ahead, trying to perfect his mastery of Zen, the days rolled into weeks and the weeks rolled into months. Upon orders from the abbot, many monks came and went, checking on the mysterious figure from time to time.

Nine years of Bodhidharma's life passed before a young monk named Shen-Kuang happened across the cave quite by chance. He had heard of the mysterious hermit that lived somewhere on the mountain, and when he noticed the outline of a figure sat in the shadows one cold winter morning, curiosity got the better of him.

Shen-Kuang approached, offering a greeting. Bodhidharma stayed silent and deathly still but his eyes were open and focused on one single spot. According to the stories the monk's brothers had once told him, the bizarre foreigner had not so much as stood up in nearly a decade.

With no acknowledgement of his presence, Shen-Kuang stepped forward to investigate. Only then, beneath the shadowy light of the cave, did he notice the two eye holes that had been burned into the far wall by Bodhidharma's gaze. Immediately, he knew this was no ordinary man.

Kneeling before Bodhidharma, the young monk begged to join him as a disciple. Once again there was no response, so he was left wondering what he could possibly do to get the mysterious figure's attention.

After kneeling in the snow outside the cave for weeks, hoping to earn the Master's respect, Shen-Kuang came to realize that he must do something spectacular to prove he was worthy.

In a display of absolute dedication, one morning he slipped away from the temple before dawn. Shen-Kuang carried a ceremonial sword on his back and, before the entrance to the cave, hacked off his own left arm at the elbow.

As his blood burned holes through the white snow, Shen-Kuang tore a strip of fabric from his robes and tied it tightly to the stump of his arm as a tourniquet. He then entered the cave and laid his bloody limb before Bodhidharma.

"The mind of your disciple is not yet quietened," he said, gritting his teeth through the tremendous pain. "I beg you Master to quiet my mind."

Coming around from his nine-year meditation, Bodhidharma answered, "Bring your mind forth and I will quieten it for you."[2]

With his formal acceptance as a Zen disciple, Bodhidharma dubbed Shen-Kuang "Hui-Ko," meaning "His wisdom is sufficient."

Over time, Bodhidharma's following grew as more monks joined Hui-Ko, curious about the teachings of Zen. Eventually, the monks invited the Great Master to take up residence in the Shaolin Temple and teach them the art of Zen Buddhism.

Finally making progress after more than a decade, Bodhidharma was pleased. One morning he was walking cheerily through the halls with the abbot when he saw several of the monks were sleeping at their stations rather than working on translating Sutras, the sacred Buddhist texts.

Bodhidharma questioned the abbot about his monks' lack of vitality, to which he responded with excuses, stating how their minds were under such demand from translating sutras and meditating that it took its toll on them physically.

Bodhidharma found this statement ridiculous, knowing full well that for one's mind to be strong, the body must be strong too. He ordered the abbot to bring his followers to the courtyard the following morning at sunrise.

The next morning, the order of monks stood in the icy, snow-covered courtyard. Bodhidharma watched for a few minutes as the group shivered, yawned, and grumbled in the cold.

Bodhidharma ordered the monks to watch him and copy his movements exactly as they saw. He first worked through a routine of yogic exercises, then the beginning of a form of unarmed fighting techniques called the "Eighteen Hands," and finally a series of breathing exercises to develop Qi. These were techniques he had learned during his time both as a child growing up in the elite warrior caste, and later as a disciple of Zen.

The monks were soon sweating and red faced but energized and awake. As they ate that morning, voices and an atmosphere of vibrancy filled the normally quiet and stoic hall.

Over time, the monks' physical and mental spirits were lifted, and they learned more techniques from Bodhidharma, including different weapon practices such as the sword, staff, and spear, and physical meditation forms that would later develop into the Shaolin style.

Similarly, the monks' focus and discipline as students of Zen Buddhism grew rapidly. Bodhidharma soon found he had a temple of skilled and dedicated followers.

Although this was not the route he had pictured, Bodhidharma found joy in the spread of his Master's teachings. For many years he remained at the temple, building his following into something greater than he could ever have imagined.

With his task finally accomplished, a yearning for his homeland swelled within Bodhidharma's aged body. In due course, he assembled his closest disciples in the cave where he had once sat for nine years. This was to be their final lesson.

Bodhidharma called forth his most devout followers one by one. Using his body as a metaphor, Bodhidharma proclaimed the depth of each of their understandings. To one he offered his skin (outer knowledge), another his flesh (deeper knowledge), and a third his bones (deeper still). Finally, calling forward Hui Ko, Bodhidharma announced, "You have got my marrow, the full depths of my teachings."[3]

Unsure how to make sense of the news that he had become the twenty-ninth patriarch of Zen Buddhism, Hui Ko prostrated himself before the Great Master and thanked him for bringing the true path of Zen to the monks of Shaolin.

THE FACTS

For years Bodhidharma's legend has been a subject of great debate. Some believe that he is a historically unfounded figure entirely, while others argue that there is clear evidence for his existence and his dissemination of Zen Buddhism and the associated Shaolin martial arts.

First, if Bodhidharma was a legitimate historical figure, the specific locations of his travels vary wildly between versions of the legend. In Southeast Asian folktales, he is stated to have traveled south by sea to Sumatra and then journeyed up the Malay Archipelago into China, teaching Buddhism and martial arts practices as he went. Some local communities consider this to have even helped pioneer the Indonesian martial art of Silat.[4]

In another version of the tale, Bodhidharma later left the Shaolin Monastery and traveled through the Korean peninsula before crossing the sea into Japan, where he is also identified as a forefather of martial arts.[5]

While his route of travel is speculative, there are various documents (albeit mostly written posthumously) that describe Bodhidharma's time in China. One notable work is "The History of the Monasteries of Luoyang," which was written in 547 CE and describes "Sramana Bodhidharma" as a Persian monk living in Yong Ning Temple and who claimed to be one-hundred-fifty years old.[6]

While there are various texts that place Bodhidharma (or another similar figure) at "Shaolin," the temple's name itself is a point of contention. In Chinese, "Shaolin" means "Young Forest" and has been used to refer to many sites throughout history, leading to conflicting theories about the actual location of the temple.

Therefore, Bodhidharma may well have been in residence at *a*, but not necessarily *the* Shaolin temple in Henan Province that is associated with him today.

Second, while Bodhidharma is often said to have established Zen Buddhism in China, some scholars believe the depiction of this lineage may have been a later undertaking to create a direct, retroactive connection between Zen and the Buddha.[7]

With this in mind, the resemblance between Bodhidharma's legend and the story of the Buddha, Siddhartha Gautama, should be noted. Both figures are said to have given up their lives of luxury as princes of the Indian Subcontinent to become wandering monks. If Bodhidharma is indeed a fictional creation, it is possible that these parallels are not coincidence.

While there are also several written Zen practices and sermons that have been posthumously accredited to Bodhidharma, the authenticity of such documents is often debated. Many modern scholars agree that these are primarily works of later Zen disciples rather than Bodhidharma himself, as the religion was not widespread until at least the seventh century.[8]

Third, the legend of Bodhidharma teaching martial arts as part of religious training may have also served a purpose for the Chinese Buddhist clergy. Historically, Buddhist monks often engaged in military crusades. The Shaolin Monks specifically served during various campaigns throughout the sixteenth and seventeenth centuries.[9]

In recent times, there may have been a drive for Chinese Buddhists to distance themselves from martial arts practices due to increased periods of peace and changes in modern religious ideologies.

One method for doing so could have been to emphasize the historical use of martial arts as purely spiritual exercises. However, Shaolin's military background appears to be a more convincing argument for hundreds of years of ongoing martial arts practice rather than being solely part of Bodhidharma's religious teachings.

It should also be noted that many drawings and sculptures of Bodhidharma from the Middle Ages portrayed him in a similar manner to any other saint or prophet—calm, good natured, and reverent. Meanwhile, the stern, bizarre-looking version of the character that we regularly see today has emerged more recently. Rubbings taken from sculptures and steles in the Shaolin temple show pronounced changes over time in both Bodhidharma's demeanor and the foreignness of his appearance when compared to Chinese saints. This is particularly noticeable from the era in which his association with martial arts became widespread.[10]

In terms of Bodhidharma's discussions with his followers, the speech in which he metaphorically offers parts of himself to his disciples—with Hui Ko "attaining the marrow," or the fundamentals of his teachings—is of particular relevance.

Many scholars throughout history have taken the term "marrow" to refer to specific texts on ancient Qigong-like practices collectively referred to as "The Marrow Cleansing Classics." However, by conservative estimates, these books did not appear until nearly one thousand years after the legend took place.[11]

Another consideration is that until around the sixteenth century, the Shaolin monks were not known for their unarmed fighting skills. Although some monks at the Shaolin temple *did* practice styles of boxing, most records indicate they used common systems of martial arts from the period rather than any specific Shaolin style.[12]

The writings of author Cheng Zhongdou (1522–1587 CE) support this, describing how at his time the monks' unarmed fighting techniques had not reached the level of their staff fighting, which was already well known.[13]

While Bodhidharma has been discussed in many texts that also reference martial arts over the centuries, there was no clear and direct link between the two, except for the occasional forged or unreliable document, until the seventeenth century.[14] In fact, the first modern incarnations of Bodhidharma's tale that resemble the one told earlier can be traced back to fiction from the early nineteenth century, one notable work being *The Travels of Lao Ts'an*, which was first published as a newspaper serial in China in 1907.[15]

Such stories were hugely popular at the time, and Bodhidharma's legend, like any good "true life" story, was nothing short of explosive. A lone traveler, a warrior mystic of great physical and spiritual power who overcame tremendous odds to complete an epic journey was compelling, just as it has been in countless other instances and cultures. In modern times, however, Bodhidharma's legend is simply more interesting and convenient than the myriad of societal, cultural, economic, and military factors that have contributed to the development of Asian martial arts traditions.

While he may be a figure of respect for Buddhists and martial artists everywhere, the known facts about Bodhidharma present a convincing argument that it is inaccurate to consider him as the father of all modern-day Asian martial arts.

Functions of the Legend

Connecting Martial Arts and Zen Philosophies

While there is sufficient evidence to suggest that Bodhidharma probably was an actual figure, or at least an amalgamation of figures who resided at one of the Shaolin Temples, it is likely that his specific exploits and teachings have been confused over the centuries, with facts, tales, and statements being misattributed.

Regardless of its authenticity, however, the legend of Bodhidharma serves an important function by connecting Zen Buddhism and the martial arts. One way it does this is by acting as a religious parable and highlighting key aspects of the Zen Buddhist teachings, such as introspection, perseverance, and physical cultivation.

For example, in Bodhidharma's conversations with Emperor Wu, it is made clear that achievements such as building temples are of lesser importance than the internal development that the Emperor has obviously neglected.

Similarly, Bodhidharma's steadfast dedication to completing his task over thousands of miles and years of his life emphasizes the strength of his spirit and perseverance required to succeed in both Buddhist practices and martial arts alike. Meanwhile his interactions with Hui-Ko reinforce this message and further teach that one must remain humble and respect one's teacher.

Furthermore, by discerning that the monks in the temple were weakened by their poor physical state and agreeing to teach them martial arts, the legend demonstrates the importance of physical cultivation for Zen Buddhists.

In Western dialogues the body and mind have historically been divided into separate entities, as described by Descartes and later revisited by Ryle, who coined the phrase "Ghost in the machine."[16] Zen Buddhism, however, teaches that these two elements are unified and work in accordance with one another.

This principle is displayed through Bodhidharma's teachings to the monks on Shaolin, and demonstrates a greater purpose for the practice of martial arts than simply to fight, tying Buddhism and martial arts practices together neatly.

Providing a Figurehead for Chinese Martial Arts

Bodhidharma's legend provides a traceable lineage for the development of Shaolin (and subsequently, all Chinese/East Asian) systems. In particular, this includes those stemming from Shaolin or that are considered to be external "hard" styles of Chinese martial arts (i.e., those that place more emphasis on strength and physical conditioning than Qi and internal alignment, such as Shaolin Kung Fu, Hung Gar, Choy-li-Fut, etc.).

Even though the Shaolin monks were historically more likely to pray to the Buddhist icon Vajrapāṇi as the divine progenitor of martial arts rather than the Buddha,[17] there have undoubtedly been many generations of Buddhist warrior monks who view Bodhidharma as their patriarch, not only in China but across Japan and Southeast Asia too.

By promoting Bodhidharma into the martial arts narrative from his original role as a Zen patriarch, a single, ancient figurehead and lineage for the practice of Shaolin Kung Fu was born.

Being ancient is often perceived as proving legitimacy for martial arts practices, even though it has been widely identified that the vast majority of "traditional" martial arts that "present themselves as ancient are hardly even old."[18] Therefore Bodhidharma's legend, at allegedly over fifteen-hundred-years-old, does a sublime job in this respect.

Promoting Chinese Martial Arts

Bodhidharma's story as a mysterious and legendary founder has certainly helped to attract students, both foreign and Chinese, to Shaolin Kung Fu and the related styles. This in turn has ensured various economic and cultural benefits for modern-day China.

By creating a traceable lineage and focal point from which all Asian martial arts (allegedly) developed, China has transformed sites such as the Shaolin Temple and the alleged cave where Bodhidharma took refuge into a Mecca for modern-day martial artists.

This has led to the creation of an entire tourism industry around the Shaolin Temple and the alleged sites Bodhidharma visited. Dozens of Buddhist and martial arts training academies are located in the surrounding region, providing "authentic Shaolin experiences" for local and international guests alike.

Similarly, Bodhidharma has now been tied so steadfastly to China, Shaolin, and the birth of Asian martial arts that it is now near impossible to separate one from the other, with Bodhidharma's role cemented within the collective consciousness of martial artists around the world.

References & Figures

[1] Adapted from Broughton, J. L. (1999). *The Bodhidharma Anthology: The Earliest Records of Zen*. University of California Press. p. 3.

[2] Broughton. (1999). p. 89.

[3] Adapted from Shahar, M. (2011). *The Shaolin Monastery: History, Religion, and the Chinese Martial Arts*. University of Hawai'i Press. p. 14.

[4] Awab, Z. A. S., & Sutton, N. (2007). *Silat Tua: The Malay Dance of Life*. Azlan Ghanie.

[5] Green, T. A. (2001). *Martial Arts of the World: An Encyclopedia*. ABC Clio. p. 126.

[6] Spiesbach, M F. (1992). "Bodhidharma: Meditating Monk, Martial Arts Master or Make-Believe?" *Journal of Asian Martial Arts* 1, no. 4: 10–27

[7] Spiesbach. (1992).

[8] Broughton, J. L. (1999). *The Bodhidharma Anthology: The Earliest Records of Zen*. University of California Press.

[9] Henning, S. E. (1981). "The Chinese Martial Arts in Historical Perspective." *Military Affairs* 45(4): 173. https://doi.org/10.2307/1987462 p. 174.

[10] Shahar, M. (2011). *The Shaolin Monastery: History, Religion, and the Chinese Martial Arts*. University of Hawai'i Press.

[11] Shahar. (2011).

[12] Henning, S. E. (1981). "The Chinese Martial Arts in Historical Perspective." Military Affairs, 45(4): 173. https://doi.org/10.2307/ 1987462.

[13] Henning. (1981).

[14] Green, T. A. (2001). *Martial Arts of the World: An Encyclopedia.* ABC Clio. p. 129.

[15] Henning, S. E. (1999). "Academia Encounters the Chinese Martial Arts." *China Review International* 6(2): 319–332. https://doi.org/10.1353/cri.1999.0020.

[16] Ryle, Gilbert. (1949). "Descartes' Myth." In *The Concept of Mind*. London: Hutchinson.

[17] Shahar, M. (2011). *The Shaolin Monastery: History, Religion, and the Chinese Martial Arts*. University of Hawai'i Press.

[18] Bowman, P. (2017). *Mythologies of Martial Arts*. Rowman and Littlefield International. p. 56.

ZHANG SANFENG
The Founding of Internal Martial Arts

Zhang Sanfeng was thought to have been born in 1247 to an affluent family in Jiangxi Province, Eastern China. When he was just five years old, a mystery disease struck Sanfeng. He lost most of his vision and was not expected to survive, although he did ultimately regain his health through the practice of Taoist techniques.

After overcoming this mystery disease, his parents sent Sanfeng to Shaolin to build up his health by studying Kung Fu for several years. He also practiced a variety of Taoist exercises for breathing and internal health.

Zhang Sanfeng is often pictured in the typical attire of Taoist monks from the era: dark robes and with a straw hat slung over his back. He is also depicted with a long mustache and beard, with his hair tied in a tight topknot.

In paintings and statues, Sanfeng is usually in seated meditation or the "cloud hands" position (i.e., stood in a wide stance with one hand placed palm-down in front of the chest while the other is opposite it at waist height, as if holding a large ball).

His date of death is unknown, and some Taoist sects consider him to be a legendary immortal. Besides being a key figure of Taoism, he is now known as the founder of Taijiquan, the Wudang martial arts legacy, and subsequently the "internal" styles of martial arts.

Over centuries, some parts of the Zhang Sanfeng legend have crossed over into the grounds of mythology, in particular from the point in which he concludes his life upon Wudang mountain and ceases to be "human." Therefore, the discussion here will focus on the story in which he creates Taijiquan, as it is widely thought to have some grounding in truth.

The Legend

It was a steep climb up the western slope of the mountain. The forest was thick and the track up to the temple was slick underfoot, the mud softened by a week-long deluge of summer rains.

At over seventy years old, Zhang Sanfeng certainly felt his age on treks like this. Still, he pushed on toward the peak, ignoring the aches in his back and legs. The old Taoist monk had spent decades training and meditating on China's highest and holiest peaks and these daily journeys, hard as they may be, helped him to focus.

As Sanfeng trudged onwards, a cool breeze blew up from the valley floor carrying the sweet aroma of sprouting young rice plants through the trees. It reminded him of the village he had left many years ago, and a touch of sadness overcame the wandering Taoist.

Part I: Spiritual Journeys

Sanfeng had no children or family to speak of, only the lessons of the great sages, warrior monks, and philosophers to give his life meaning. Many years had passed as he searched for the true path to peace and enlightenment, but he was no closer now than he had been when he started.

The lower limbs of a great white pine tree snagged Sanfeng's robe as he pushed past them and into a clearing. The hot summer sun was spilling through the gaps in the branches overhead. Just then, a flash of movement in the center of the glade caught his attention.

Creeping forward, Sanfeng strained to make out what was happening; his vision was not all it once had been. From twenty yards away, he realized what he was seeing.

In the middle of the clearing, perched atop an enormous granite boulder, a crane was flapping its wings and stabbing its beak downward. At the bird's feet, a snake coiled on the rock as it attempted to defend itself from the onslaught of attacks. With his presence unnoticed by the two creatures engaged in a battle of life and death, Sanfeng watched intently.

As the crane lunged, the serpent would rock back out of range on its tail, building up energy in its powerful torso. The snake would then return the blow, shooting forward ferociously like an arrow from a bow. A moment before the attacker's teeth found its limb, the crane would raise its leg, sweep the strike away with a downward arc from its wing, and counter with its own attack.

Sanfeng stayed close, watching the back-and-forth dance of death. He was enamored; neither animal seemed to tire or lose focus. It was as if they knew each other's only weakness and could go on battling this way endlessly until one or the other made a fatal mistake.

Finally, with neither creature gaining the upper hand, the crane decided it was going to look for an easier meal and flew off. The snake slithered away into the undergrowth. Just like that, the battle was over. The old monk wondered how such different creatures, opposites like light and dark, could be so evenly matched.

Sanfeng removed his straw hat, wiped the sweat from his brow, and sat down on the warm stone to ponder the question. Linear strikes had been met with circular responses and vice versa; strength had been met with yielding action, and aggression had been met with calm.

After a few minutes of silence, Sanfeng began to laugh as he sat alone in the clearing, wondering why it had taken a lifetime for him to see something so obvious. This duality was everywhere, clear as night and day, hot and cold, life, and death. It was the essence of the universe and, with some work, it could be his path to creating unifying peace.

Following the moment of illuminating truth that Sanfeng had spent almost an entire lifetime questing for, the old man forgot about his aching legs. He half ran the remaining mile to the temple on the western peak.

That evening, under candlelight, he frantically made notes and sketches of the concepts he had seen. Now, though, he felt uncertain whether he had simply been lost in watching two animals battle or if a pair of great Taoist spirits themselves had been communicating with him using these creatures as their vessels.

* * *

From that point onward, Sanfeng combined this dualistic principle of combat with the internal energy training of his Taoist methods. He developed sequences like those he'd learned during the years he had spent in Shaolin, adapting the techniques that had proved effective in his decades of wandering a dangerous land.

Sanfeng spent the next few years working obsessively on his new system. The Taoist monk studied nature, herbalism, alchemy, and meditation, incorporating a lifetime of lessons into the principles and philosophy of what would soon become known as "The Supreme Ultimate Fist."

As he refined each technique, the monk tested them out against the martial Taoist sects in the monasteries on Mount Wudang.

It was there he developed what he called the "Thirteen Posture Form" and taught it to the monks to aid their safety, longevity, and spiritual vitality.

Once his development was complete, Sanfeng left Mount Wudang to spread his teachings far and wide. His "Supreme Ultimate Fist" would be a martial art for those too weak or frail to defend themselves against the violence and hate that was rife throughout their lands. It would be a tool for his people to better themselves physically, mentally, and spiritually. Taijiquan would be Sanfeng's gift to the world.

THE FACTS

While Zhang Sanfeng is revered as both a patron of Taoism and Taijiquan, there are several facts about his legend that remain unknown or that have become convoluted over the ages.

First, it is often claimed that Zhang Sanfeng was born in 1247, but there is little evidence to support this. The most likely reason for this date being chosen is its occurrence in the 1960s newspaper serial "The Heavenly Sword and Dragon Saber," which helped repopularize his tale.[1]

Alternative tellings of the story claim that he lived anywhere between 960 and 1644. Although this does not necessarily cast doubt on Sanfeng's existence, it shows that verifiable historical records surrounding the figure are sadly lacking.

Stories of Zhang Sanfeng's early life regularly describe him as a sickly and weak child, who almost lost his eyesight to a mystery illness in his youth (if so, polio is a likely suspect). Often it is said that the aura of Sanfeng's Qi caught the attention of a wandering monk, who then helped cure him by harnessing his internal strength through Taoist exercises. Then after the boy's health improved, his parents sent him to build up his strength further by training at the Shaolin Temple.[2]

However, with no records of Sanfeng's youth other than those written when his tale grew popular in the twentieth century, this history should be considered a modern creation.

The first factual information we have about Sanfeng comes from records of the Wudang mountain monasteries. These show that there was not just one, but two Sanfengs who made their homes upon the mountain.

This could be a plausible explanation for reported sightings of him over the course of two hundred years, and the confusion surrounding his birth date.[3]

The first Sanfeng lived in the twelfth century, and was a Taoist monk who allegedly hid on the mountain to seek refuge from a band of outlaws to whom he owed money. It is said that the concept of Taijiquan, or the hard-soft fast-slow dynamic, later came to this Sanfeng in a dream (sometimes including the crane and snake as a vision). He then developed the style to fend off the enemies that eventually tracked him down.

The second Sanfeng lived in Wudang during the fourteenth century and appears to have been the more eccentric of the two. He was seen as a "mad alchemist"[4] hunting for immortality. The link between this figure and the crane and snake, which both traditionally represent longevity in Chinese culture, is therefore immediately apparent.

Many Taijiquan practitioners trace lineages back to Sanfeng (usually via the Chen family of Chenjiagou village in Henan province, which lies approximately one-hundred-sixty miles north of Wudang). Most of these lineages, however, are based upon speculation rather than verifiable history.

In fact, some scholars claim that Sanfeng never existed as a real-life historical figure and that he was originally a Taoist immortal with little or no ties to martial arts. In this case, it is possible that his legend was simply appropriated during the early twentieth century when anti-superstition campaigns of the era posed a threat to such activities. Taijiquan is thought to have then followed in the footsteps of other cult-like practices that were "de-spirited and re-mythologized to fit the living-hero model."[5]

Due to a century-long prohibition of martial arts and purging of historical documents by Emperor Qianlong, many records from between 1550 and 1750 were destroyed.[6] However, the Chen clan had family histories of martial arts tracing back to the fourteenth century. These began with Chen Bu and were then passed down through eight generations to Chen Wang

Ting, a decorated military officer who formalized "Chen Style" Taijiquan.[7]

One point of debate surrounding this lineage is that the early Chen style bears a striking number of similarities to an amalgamated Chinese martial art system of thirty-two movements developed by General Qi Jiguang (1528–1587), a noted military martial arts expert of the day.

While twenty-five of the original Chen-Style movements occur in Qi Jiguang's manual, there are several other techniques that do not, but instead appear in records from the nearby Shaolin temple.[8] Some scholars however, argue that these similarities are coincidental.[9]

There are also many similarities between the Chen style and techniques developed marginally earlier in the nearby Zhaobao Village, which also trace their roots back to Sanfeng. This suggests possible shared influences between the two. Regardless, the first verifiable histories of Taijiquan appear in the seventeenth century, stemming from Wenxian County in Henan Province and are considered to "represent the beginnings of all major forms of Taijiquan."[10]

While none of these points establish with any certainty that Zhang Sanfeng was or wasn't the creator of Taijiquan (as he also allegedly trained in Shaolin styles), they show at the very least that similar practices were already taking place elsewhere in the country, and suggests at least partial influences from other sources.

The earliest written account that related Sanfeng to martial arts as more than simply a Taoist sage was in the book *Epitaph for Wang Zhengnan*. This text was published in 1669— significantly, after the beginning of the Chen Family records.

Although there was no specific mention of the term Taijiquan in *Epitaph*, the author Huang Zongxi was the first to categorize martial arts into the classifications of "internal" and "external," listing Sanfeng as the patriarch of the former. This coincidentally also gave birth to the divide between Chinese martial arts that has lasted for centuries and is still a topic of contention today.[11]

Although the written account of Sanfeng as a martial artist has been taken as gospel by many historians and martial arts practitioners, others believe that Zongxi did not write the text as a historical resource but rather as a political allegory. The division of Chinese martial arts into "internal" and "external" schools, represented by the rival Wudang and Shaolin traditions respectively, was a metaphor for the ousted Ming Dynasty and the ruling Manchu government (of whom Zongxi was a vocal opponent).[12]

The "external" Shaolin boxing school represented foreign Buddhism and, as a result, the Manchu government, exemplifying them as outsiders. Conversely, the Ming were represented by the "internal" practices of Taoism and the Wudang Schools. This painted the internal martial arts as native or indigenous practices that should be embraced more wholly than foreign practices (and, by association, rulers and religion).

It wasn't until much later that Zhang Sanfeng was associated with the name "Taijiquan" directly, rather than the vague category of internal martial arts.

This was first recorded in the "Brief Preface to Taijiquan," published in 1867, which accredited Sanfeng as the founder of the system.[13] Interestingly, the author later retracted this statement in a second edition and instead claimed the founder was unknown. Some suggest that it may have been due to the

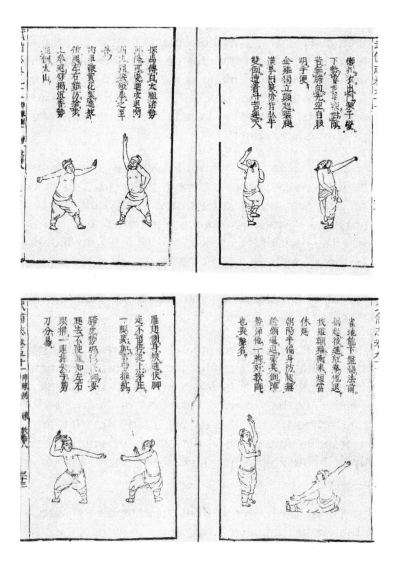

Excerpts from General Qi Jiguang's *New Book of Military Efficiency* published in 1584, showing a number of movements with similarities to modern-day Taijiquan, such as the "single whip."

author's own acceptance of the spurious nature of his tale.[14] But by this time, the story was out and could not be reined in.

According to Henning, Sanfeng's evolution from Taoist immortality seeker to the creator of Taijiquan should be considered in three stages: prior to 1670 when he was known as a revered Taoist saint; after 1670 when he was labeled as the founder of internal martial arts; and after 1900 when he was upgraded to the patriarch of Taijiquan.[15]

As with any legend of this age, there is a lack of evidence that could conclusively verify or dispute claims around Sanfeng's life or practices. However, there is enough to suggest that he may have been an actual figure, albeit one who was only identified as a Taoist saint until relatively recent times.

While there is good reason for many Taijiquan practitioners to trace the lineages of their style back through the Chen family to Sanfeng, it appears that these are often cases of eisegesis or confirmation bias, in which those looking hard enough for a pathway back to such a figure will inevitably find one.

As a result of this inconclusive information, it is difficult to either confirm or deny that Zhang Sanfeng had any considerable influence over the development of the art we now call Taijiquan. From the known facts, however, it appears more realistic that numerous martial artists devised the system over time as an eclectic amalgamation of Shaolin, Taoist, and other family systems of martial arts, rather than as the sole creation of a single person.

FUNCTIONS OF THE LEGEND

Providing Rationale for the Practice of Taijiquan

Although research shows that it is likely Zhang Sanfeng was not the sole creator of Taijiquan, his legend serves to highlight some of the key principles and purposes of training in the system.

There are numerous martial elements within Taijiquan that can effectively be applied to fighting; however, the health and longevity benefits of the system are displayed more prominently in the legend. Sanfeng embodies these principles perfectly, beginning his "true" training as an old man and then going on to become more-or-less immortal through his practice.

While it is unlikely that many modern-day practitioners of Taijiquan are suddenly going to attain immortality, there is a plethora of research that conclusively shows the health benefits of Taijiquan, particularly in relation to longevity and benefits for older practitioners.

Furthermore, the concept of *Qi* and the use of this mystical element for healing is understood differently by different groups. A recent medical view of *Qi* as the culmination of breathing, mental focus, and body mechanics gives an example of how this training is highly advantageous.

Teaching the Physical and Spiritual Aspects of Taijiquan

Sanfeng's legend also serves as a valuable learning tool, using the examples of the crane and the snake to teach important lessons about the structure and form of Taijiquan itself.

In particular, the legend highlights principles of Yin and Yang/hard and soft movements that are fundamental in both the physical and spiritual practices of Taijiquan.

The legend also serves as a counterbalance to the Zen orthodox traditions highlighted by Bodhidharma, Shaolin, and the external martial arts. It provides rationale and reasoning for the development and ongoing practice of the "internal" soft styles of martial arts that emphasize features such as breathing, posture, and the development of Qi (e.g., Taijiquan, Xingyiquan, and Baguazhang). This rationale primarily being spiritual development (in the form of Taoism) and physical benefits, rather than pure martial efficacy or Buddhist purposes.

While Sanfeng's legend is obviously not meant to be literal, the principles that underpin it allow us to further understand our own practices and reap the benefits of that come from the practice of Taijiquan. These include better health, better mental faculties, *some* practical martial arts skills, and a deeper understanding of the surrounding history and culture.

Providing a Figurehead for Taijiquan

Sanfeng's legend creates a single historical figurehead for the system rather than attributing its development and refinement to numerous practitioners over time. This version of the events grew to popularity in the twentieth century, and likely appealed (and continues to appeal) to followers of Taijiquan who have preconceptions of an exotic and ancient system of martial arts.

Possibly because of the vast variety of media, such as film, television, books, and oral histories that discuss Sanfeng and the historical development of Taijiquan, there is what Adam Frank calls a clear "romanticization of the past that intensifies with each generation."[16] Surprisingly, the appeal of this ancient and mysterious history, embodied as it is by Sanfeng, is not just present among western audiences, but also within China and throughout Asia.

References & Figures

[1] Liu. X (2018, August 7). *Zhang Sanfeng: A Semi-Mythical Chinese Taoist Priest.* Retrieved November 24, 2021, http://en.chinaculture.org/2018-08/07/content_589708.htm.

[2] *Zhang Sanfeng* (张三丰), "Founder of Tai Chi: The Extraordinary Story of a Mysterious Hero." *The Epoch Times* (Singapore). (2019, January 3). Retrieved November 24, 2021, from https://epochtimes.today/zhang-sanfeng-张三丰-founder-of-tai-chi-the-extraordinary-story-of-a-mysterious-hero/.

[3] Green, T. A. (2001). *Martial Arts of the World: An Encyclopedia.* ABC Clio. p. 618.

[4] Green. *Martial Arts of the World*. (2001). p. 648.

[5] Phillips, S. P. (2019). "The Zhang Sanfeng Conundrum: Taijiquan and Ritual Theater." *Journal of Daoist Studies* 12(1): 96–122.

https://doi.org/10.1353/dao.2019.0004. p. 99.

[6] Henning, S. (1994). "Ignorance, Legend and Taijiquan." *Journal of the Chen Style Taijiquan Research Association of Hawaii* 2(3): 1–7.

[7] Chen, M. (2004). *Old Frame Chen Family Taijiquan*. North Atlantic Books.

[8] Henning, S. (1981). "The Chinese Martial Arts in Historical Perspective." *Military Affairs* 45 4) 173–79. https://doi.org/10.2307/1987462. p. 174.

[9] Phillips. (2019). The Zhang Sanfeng Conundrum. p. 100.

[10] Green. *Martial Arts of the World*. (2001). p. 620.

[11] Henning. (1981). p. 174.

[12] Green, T. A. (2001). *Martial Arts of the World: An Encyclopedia*. ABC Clio. p. 618.

[13] Sim, D. S.-V., & Gaffney, D. (2002). *Chen Style Taijiquan: The Source of Taiji Boxing*. North Atlantic Books.

[14] Sim & Gaffney. *Chen Style Taijiquan*. p. 28

[15] Henning, S. (1994*).* "Ignorance, Legend, and Taijiquan." *Journal of the Chen Style Taijiquan Research Association of Hawaii*, 2(3): 1–7.

[16] Quoted in Bowman, P. (2017). *Mythologies of Martial Arts*. Rowman et Littlefield International. p. 37.

Page 30 drawing adapted from Qi, J. (1584). *New Book of Military Efficiency (Ji Xiao Xin Shu* 紀效新書). (J. Chen, trans.).

MORIHEI UESHIBA
The Quest for Ultimate Peace

Morihei Ueshiba was born on December fourteenth, 1883, to a well-respected family in Tanabe, a coastal city in southern Japan. Among five siblings, he was the only son. As a child, Ueshiba was weak and bookish, so his father led him to martial arts, hoping to develop his health and spirit.

As a young man, he was known to have trained in Kenjutsu (swordsmanship) and Bojutsu (staff fighting), Daito-Ryu, Akijutsu, Judo, and Sumo wrestling.

Ueshiba was known for his small stature and unassuming appearance. This paired well with his peaceful ethos, and often led him to surprise others with his strength. While commonly seen pictures of Ueshiba come from late in his life and show him as thin and bald with a long gray beard, embodying the wise old sage character perfectly, in his youth he was reasonably muscular.

Ueshiba died on April twenty-sixth, 1969. His ashes were enshrined in the family temple in Tanabe. Every year, his followers hold a memorial service at the Aiki Shrine in Iwama.

He is now known as *O' Sensei* (Great Master), the founder and patriarch of Aikido. He is the author of *The Way of Peace* and recipient of the Japanese Medal of Honor (Purple Ribbon), Order of the Rising Sun, and Order of the Sacred Treasure.

Morihei Ueshiba is a very well-known figure in Japan, and indeed, the world. His life has been well documented in written works, both autobiographical and otherwise, and he has developed an almost cult-like following. This has led to a great deal of mystery, exaggeration, and elaboration surrounding some particular events of his life.

THE LEGEND

The rope cut deep into his wrists as a squad of soldiers marched Morihei Ueshiba and his brothers of the Omoto-Kyo Shinto sect across the firing range. Bullet holes pockmarked the landscape and half-rotten corpses were strewn across the field, stinking like death and swarming with clouds of fat black flies.

Had it been a mistake following his teacher, Onisaburo Deguchi, on his quest for the fabled Buddhist kingdom of Shambhala? It was certainly starting to feel so.

The gray clouds were thick overhead. Ueshiba was certain the rains would wash their blood away in time, leaving no trace that the band of pacifists and holy men had ever set foot in this cold and dangerous land.

Ueshiba watched as the man to his left, another follower of Onisaburo and the Omoto-Kyo sect, refused the blindfold. With a soft shake of his head, Ueshiba let the Chinese soldier know that he too intended to face death head on.

The young soldier returned to the line of his peers and shouldered his weapon. An officer shouted a command. Safety catches clicked off. Ueshiba offered a silent prayer to the heavens, and a ray of golden light cracked through the matted gray clouds above.

A moment before the signal came to fire, another officer came running across the range, waving a piece of faded yellow paper in his hand and shouting as he went.

The seconds that followed made no sense at all. There were a few barked commands. The firing squad lowered their weapons.

Moments later, Ueshiba's and his colleagues' wrists were untied. They were free! But why? Had it been divine intervention?

The commander approached the row of Omoto-Kyo disciples, still standing half-frozen in shock. He stopped before Onisaburo, who was somehow still wearing a casual smile, and the pair talked in hushed tones for a few seconds.

Shortly after, the group's horses were led back across the range and returned. The commander then waved them away nonchalantly, as if dismissing an annoying child. Without needing to be told twice, Ueshiba and his fellow disciples sped off in a blind gallop west.

But their freedom was to be short-lived. Only a few days of rough sleeping and drinking from streams went by before they were back in harm's way. Squads of the Chinese military were tracking them. Maybe it was the same men from before who had changed their minds about releasing their prisoners, or could it be others? There was no way to know.

The group, exhausted and weakened by their hardships, were finally pinned down in a valley, as the enemy started firing upon them from the north and east. It was only a matter of time before someone took a bullet.

Just when all seemed hopeless, an epiphany struck Ueshiba. In that instant, he realized that his mission was one of divine purpose; it was the reason he'd walked away from the firing squad, and it was how he and the Omoto-Kyo followers would walk away from this encounter too.

In a moment of grand illumination, he could suddenly see the paths of the bullets as they tore through the air and thudded into the ground at his feet. Each shot's trajectory glowed, marked by a glorious golden beam of light.

Ueshiba pulled his reins hard and charged away from the gunfire. He raced forward, leading the group on a path visible only to him through the beams, until they emerged over the ridgeline of the valley without so much as a scratch upon them.

Ueshiba had now faced his own mortality twice and emerged from the experiences with a profound understanding of life and death.

* * *

Upon his return to Japan, Ueshiba knew he must fulfill his destiny as a man of peace. By using the systems of Daito-Ryu Karate and Aikijutsu that he had studied intensively since his childhood, Ueshiba set about creating a system of martial arts based on the spiritual goals of the Omoto-Kyo. It was to be an art for the development of oneself rather than the oppression or domination of others.

Ueshiba called his system Aikido, meaning the "Way of Harmonious Spirit." Eventually, the Master's profile grew to the point where challengers would come from all over Japan to his dojo in Ayabe Prefecture. More often than not, Ueshiba would knock his opponent down without even being touched. He would then give them a quick lecture on the meaning of peace and send them on their way better off for the experience. However, one challenger was different.

It was a hot summer afternoon when a high-ranking Kendo fighter and naval officer arrived at Ueshiba's modest Dojo. He arrogantly demanded a duel and refused to leave until he got one. The Aikido Master could tell this was a man of pride, one who had never tasted defeat and could not be dissuaded with words alone.

Intrigued by the man and curious of his skills, Ueshiba agreed to a duel and drew his wooden weapon from the rack on the far wall. The officer gave him a slight bow and offered a few empty pleasantries, which the Aikido Master returned with a warm smile.

The Kendo fighter charged first, swinging at Ueshiba with a flurry of fast sword strikes but hit only air. Frustrated by his failing efforts, the swordsman lashed out furiously again and again as if he were trying to take Ueshiba's head off. Soon, his arms became like lead weights, and the chance of him even touching the Aikido master disappeared. Exhausted and unable to comprehend what had passed, the officer finally conceded defeat and dropped his weapon.

Ueshiba kneeled down beside the swordsman. He told him that even though the fighter's spirit was strong, his cuts were fast, and his power phenomenal, the idea of winning or losing was nothing more than an illusion. He explained that if the Kendo fighter could attain harmony with the universe, he too would possess such power, seeing his attacker's intentions as beams of golden light before he even knew them himself.

Rising to his feet, Ueshiba walked out into the garden to the stone well to pull up a pail of water. As he moved, a second moment of euphoric transcendence came upon him, much like he had felt under fire in the valley, only now it was infinitely stronger.

The earth seemed to tremble. Golden vapor welled up from the ground and engulfed him. All at once, Ueshiba understood the nature of creation: the true way of the warrior was to manifest love and develop a spirit that embraces and nurtures all things. From that point onward, all attachments he felt to material things vanished and Ueshiba knew he was now purely a prophet of peace.[1]

THE FACTS

First, it should be acknowledged that Japan has a long history of cult-like followings, especially surrounding spiritual practices such as Shintoism (a religion in which followers worship deities/spirits connected to certain places or people).[2] This history may assist us in understanding both how Ueshiba was influenced and how he gained such a significant following and status in relatively recent times.

Onisaburo, the leader of the Omoto-Kyo sect and initiator of the missions to locate the fabled "Promised Land of Shambhala," is often considered the spiritual forefather of Aikido's philosophy. However, historical records paint him in a less favorable light.

Despite being a polymath who excelled in spirituality, psychology, art, and poetry, and who spoke several languages, many considered Onisaburo to be a conman. At one point, he was openly labeled "the biggest charlatan in history," and a childhood friend stated that, "It was impossible to tell if he was a genius or a fool."[3] However, given that he led an overland adventure on horseback in search of a mythical kingdom in a war-torn Chinese Republic that still harbored fresh memories of Japanese occupation, this author would suspect the latter.

In regard to the miraculous escape of Ueshiba and his associates from the firing squad, some scholars suspect the Chinese had no intention of executing their prisoners. They posit that this was either a scare tactic or an attempt to curry favor from the Japanese by saving and returning Onisaburo, who was already a popular public figure.[4]

In some versions of Ueshiba's story, it is claimed that the weapons of the Chinese were faulty. However, it seems improbable that the Chinese army could not produce half a dozen working rifles during wartime.

As for Ueshiba's tale of escape by dodging bullets, there are several accounts from members of the Omoto-Kyo sect confirming that the army did indeed attack them. However, similarly to the feigned execution, this could have been a scare tactic or a display of power for the foreigners, with intentionally inaccurate warning shots.

If the Chinese military had seriously been attempting to stop the Japanese pilgrims from escaping, it is unlikely that they would have failed to hit a single member of the group when firing down upon them from several vantage points. However, it is still possible that it was simply a lucky coincidence that spared Ueshiba and his companions.

As Omoto-Kyo records mirror Ueshiba's descriptions, it seems likely that, intentionally or not, the group constructed a shared narrative of what happened through their discussions of the experience.

Onisaburo, Ueshiba (second and third from the left) and other Omoto-Kyo followers in shackles after their arrest in Mongolia.

It has been demonstrated that psychological disorders such as PTSD drastically affect the way in which stressful scenarios are recalled.[5] The notion of invincibility (believing that it is impossible for others to harm you, and a resulting willingness to take part in dangerous behaviors) is a well-documented phenomenon among war veterans and those who have been exposed to extreme violence and death.[6]

Although posthumously diagnosing a historical figure with a psychological disorder is uncertain and inadvisable (nor would this author be qualified to do so), many symptoms seen in modern-day war veterans are suspiciously similar to those described by the Aikido master.

In regard to Ueshiba's duel with the Kendo practitioner, while it is impossible to know his internal experience except from his own writings, it is recorded that he "gave different accounts of the event over the years, and, in his old age, seems to have gradually fused several separate incidents together to form this final version."[7]

Finally, as Ueshiba's cult-hero status grew throughout Japan and the rest of the world, a wealth of other unsubstantiated and often outrageous myths were also attributed to him. For example, he could throw entire groups of attackers using only one finger (or sometimes none at all), predict the future, speak with animals, and even teleport. Some of these myths he denied, while others he seemed to embrace.[8]

Functions of the Legend

Elevating Ueshiba's Status

The founder of Aikido was, without a doubt, an excellent martial artist and human being who worked with fervor to create a more peaceful world. However, many of the legends surrounding him are somewhat spurious and, in certain cases, downright dangerous.

While the divine or magical aspects of Ueshiba's legend seem ridiculous (at least to the skeptic), they serve an important function, elevating him to a mythical status among followers of the Omoto-Kyo religion and many Aikido martial arts practitioners. Even today, many still consider him to have been literally invincible.[9]

Having this type of figurehead in a martial arts system is obviously desirable (who wouldn't want to learn from someone so skilled they were impossible to defeat?) In this way, it is a very convenient tool for drawing people toward a martial art deemed mysterious and inexplicable.

Teaching the Physical Aspects of Aikido

Many masters of Aikido understand that Ueshiba's martial philosophies, such as avoiding violence whenever possible, represent the true nature of his teachings, and that they grew out of his experiences in violent and hostile situations.

However, these philosophies may be misrepresented in practice. Of course, as a lifelong martial artist and war veteran Ueshiba obviously knew about the realities of self-defense.

As a result, his system *does* contain practical fighting elements, and what is often misconstrued by observers to be impossible throwing techniques are often grounded in more functional applications, such as creating openings to strike with bare hands, knife or sword.

However, in extreme cases, Aikido's pacifistic ideals encourage practitioners to avoid any physical confrontation, even in training. This means that many techniques are never tried or tested for realism against resisting opponents (let alone those actively fighting back), but simply assumed to be functional.

A practitioner who has only ever seen his art used with total effectiveness against a passive and primed opponent (or even worse, one that has been led to believe each of their techniques will be effective at throwing or controlling a much larger and more aggressive enemy), will be ill-prepared for any actual violent confrontation.

Conversely, however, Ueshiba's legend displays the key features of the physical practice of Aikido, which are not focused on military-style combat readiness. Instead, Aikido often employs non-confrontational responses to aggression, avoiding the direct path of attack, redirecting force instead of meeting it head on, and controlling the aggressor's balance and distance to overcome their attack.

From my own experiences with Aikido, I can attest that although not necessarily the most practical martial art in terms of pure fighting skill, it is undoubtedly beneficial for a number of physical and mental faculties. I would argue that the improved physical awareness and fitness along with concentration, focus, and many other mental benefits that stem from training Aikido are the key aspects emphasized by Ueshiba's legend.

Teaching the Spiritual Aspects of Aikido

The prophet-like quest of Ueshiba may also serve as a parable for his followers, displaying a number of important spiritual aspects that should be found among Buddhists, Shintoists, and martial artists alike.

For example, Ueshiba's perseverance and commitment is highlighted through his dedication to his teacher and their journey despite untold hardships and challenges. Similarly, pacifism in the face of violence and constantly striving to better oneself are cornerstones of his legend and later teachings alike.

Additionally, the nonexclusive nature of the Omoto-Kyo religion and Aikido are also key teachings of Ueshiba's legend. Followers of either are traditionally not required to commit themselves to a single religion or martial arts lineage (as they may have been with other institutions throughout history). Instead, they are encouraged to participate freely, in the hope that their involvement will produce positive results on some level.

An Aikido instructor uses a circular, evasive technique to off-balance and throw his training partner rather than meeting his force head on.

References & Figures

[1]Adapted from Ueshiba, M., & Stevens, J. (2018). *The Art of Peace*. Shambhala. p. 1.

[2] Teeuwen, M. (2007). Comparative Perspectives on the Emergence of Jindō and Shinto. *Bulletin of the School of Oriental and African Studies 70*(2): 373–402. https://doi.org/10.1017/s0041977x07000456. p. 347.

[3] Stevens, J. (1999). *Invincible Warrior: An Illustrated Biography of Morihei Ueshiba, Founder of Aikido*. Shambhala.

[4] Stevens. (1999).

[5] Lents, N. H. (2016, May 23). "Trauma, PTSD, and Memory Distortion." *Psychology Today*. Retrieved October 20, 2018, from https://www.psychologytoday.com/us/blog/beastly-behavior/201605/trauma-ptsd-and-memory-distortion

[6] Killgore, W. D. S., et al. (2008). "Post-Combat Invincibility: Violent Combat Experiences Are Associated with Increased Risk-Taking Propensity Following Deployment." *Journal of Psychiatric Research* 42(13): 1112–1121. https://doi.org/10.1016/j.jpsychires.2008.01.001.

[7] Stevens, J. (1999). p. 81.

[8] Thomas, B. (2007). *Immortal Combat: Portrait of a True Warrior*. Blue Snake Books.

[9] Stone, J., & Meyer, R. C. (1995). *Aikido in America*. North Atlantic Books.

Page 42 photo is a public domain image.

Page 46 photo from the author's personal collection.

Part II

REBELLION TALES

The legends found here primarily come from times of military, religious, or social oppression, when warriors were forced to stand up to their overlords and, in doing so, immortalize themselves as heroes of martial arts.

As a result, many of these legends in particular have found a place in nationalistic versions of events that support the freedom, dominance, or development of a country or people. This has, in the author's opinion at least, led to a significant number of liberties being taken with the facts over time. However, it has also imbued many of the legends with strong purposes and functions that are relevant to their modern-day followers.

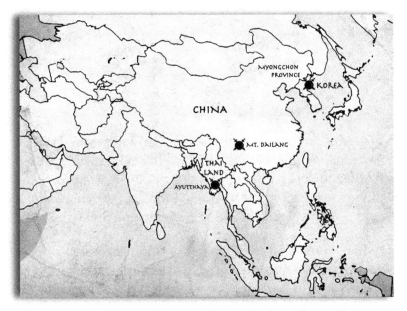

Key sites from Chapter Two: Ayutthaya (Modern Thailand), Mount Dailang, China and Myongchon Province in North Korea.

NG MUI AND YAN YONGCHUN
The Dual Founders of Wing Chun

Ng Mui, known as Wu Mei in Mandarin, was born in China in approximately 1703. Little is known about her early life; however, it is often claimed that she trained in the Southern Shaolin Temple from a young age, studying Shaolin Kung Fu, White Crane, and Southern Dragon Style.

Ng Mui is rarely pictured in paintings or historical records of Wing Chun. As a nun, she is likely to have had a shaved head and dressed in dark orange or blue-gray robes typical of the Buddhist practitioners of the era.

She is known as one of five elders of the Southern Shaolin Temple, the matriarch of Wing Chun Kuen (The Eternal Springtime Fist) and teacher of Yan Yongchun.

While there are few (if any) concrete historical records relating to Ng Mui, her legend forms such a fundamental part of

Wing Chun's background that she must be included in any discussion on the development of the system.

Ng Mui is said to have been a nun at the Southern Shaolin Temple who escaped when the ruling Qing Dynasty razed the complex for harboring Ming loyalists, many of whom were martial arts experts. Legend states that in a similar situation to Zhang Sanfeng, Ng Mui developed the early principles of Wing Chun by watching a snake fighting a crane. She focused on using sharp, lethal attacks to overcome an enemy's size and weight advantage.

* * *

Yan Yongchun, or Yim Wing Chun in Mandarin, is said to have been born around 1735 in a village at the foot of the Dailang Mountains in Southwest Sichuan Province. Her mother died at a young age, so she was raised by her father, a village tofu seller named Yan Si.

Yan Yongchun is described as being a petite and beautiful young woman in her early twenties at the time the story takes place. She is said to have trained in early forms of Wing Chun Kuen, White Crane, and Southern Dragon (under Ng Mui). She is known for refining and spreading an early form of modern Wing Chun along with her husband and being the namesake of the system.

Although initially developed from Ng Mui's teachings, Yan Yongchun's physical attributes, contributions, and circumstances are said to have played an important role in the development of Wing Chun and its later dissemination.

Also, while one of the key components of this legend is a duel, I have considered this legend as a Rebellion Tale due to the ongoing themes of resistance that occur in both Ng Mui and Yim Wing Chun's stories.

THE LEGEND

It was a warm spring morning when Ng Mui made her way down from the White Crane Temple on Mount Dailang, a place that had become her second home since Southern Shaolin was razed by fire in years prior. By now, the villagers knew the nun well as she often ventured down to purchase supplies for the Buddhist disciples that lived in the temple.

Mui's last stop today was at the shop of a tofu seller named Yan Si. She would often chat with the friendly older man, and as time passed, she got to know him and his daughter well.

When Mui entered the shady, wood-walled shack, there was no sign of Yan Si. Instead she found his daughter, a pretty young woman named Yongchun, stooped over the counter with her head in her hands, sobbing.

Yan Si's daughter looked up through puffy red eyes and the nun felt it was her duty to help. Mui asked what was troubling her and the young woman explained her predicament.

It seemed a local gang leader had taken an interest in Yongchun and had been hanging around in the village, pestering her while she tried her best to politely ignore his advances. He and his men were already threatening and extorting half the community, and that morning the thug had publicly announced he was going to make Yongchun his wife and kill anyone who tried to stop him.

The young woman was heartbroken at the prospect of being forced to marry the thug rather than the man she loved. Leung Bok Chau was a traveling salt merchant and martial artist who came through the village a few times each year.

He and Yongchun had been friends since childhood and hoped to marry soon, but it seemed her dreams had been dashed. Taking pity on the young woman, Ng Mui agreed to help Yongchun.

When the gangster returned to the village a few days later for his weekly collection of bribes and extortion money, Ng Mui was waiting in the tofu shop. The moment he tried to put his hands on Yongchun she stepped forward, blocking his path. Before he had a chance to lash out, Mui spoke. "Let's make a deal."

The thug paused, his interest piqued by the old nun before him. Surely she couldn't have owned anything of value, could she? "What kind of deal?"

"I'm Yongchun's teacher. If you can beat my student in a fight six months from today, she will go with you freely. If she wins, she gets to stay."[1]

The gangster roared with laughter, his cronies copying him from the doorway. After a few seconds, the ruckus quieted down. He was in a predicament. The thug couldn't look scared to fight a girl in front of his men, so he couldn't refuse, but it was a long time to wait. On the other hand, if he won her fair and square, it would definitely make things easier. The gangster finally shook the nun's hand, vowing to return in six months and claim his prize.

Yongchun was aghast. "What have you got me into? I'm finished now," she said.[2] She knew nothing about fighting. How was she going to fight a cruel, violent thug in a matter of months? It looked like her life was as good as over.

Mui took charge of the situation and bid Yan Si farewell, leading his daughter from the village up into the mountains and to the safety of the temple.

The nun, seeing how small and weak Yongchun was, decided to train her in a new style of martial arts she had been developing for just such occasions as this.

* * *

Almost six months to the day passed before Ng Mui led her student back down the mountain. As the pair strode into the square, the villagers met them with wide eyes. The timid, pretty Yongchun seemed to have vanished, and in her place walked a confident young woman with her back straight and her head up, unafraid to be the subject of their attention.

The thought of seeing her father once again overwhelmed Yongchun, and her heart fluttered when she learned that her love, Leung Bok Chau, would soon return on his annual trip to the village. Now, there was just one obstacle in her way.

For a few days, all was quiet. Yongchun cleaned and helped her father, who looked as though he'd aged a decade since she left. The stress of running his business alone and the constant threats from the gangsters had been almost too much for him to handle.

The warm fall sun was high in the sky when voices coming from the street caught Yongchun's attention. She glanced over from behind the counter to where her father was resting after preparing his wares for the day. His eyes widened with fear.

The thug strolled in through the shop doors, flanked by a group of his men. His flat, broken nose and stained yellow teeth made him look even more revolting than Yongchun remembered.

He seemed much bigger and more intimidating now too. A shiver of apprehension crept down her spine.

Without a word, Yongchun took off her apron and paced out toward the village square, while the gangster and his men followed her, leering and laughing all the way.

The villagers poured out into the streets at the sound of the ruckus, half curious, half fearful over what was taking place. A circle formed around them in the dusty street.

Her would-be husband rolled up his sleeves and strutted into the center of the space, ready for what he expected to be a quick and easy victory. Yongchun stepped forward; he grinned and raised his fists, wondering if she was actually going to go through with this ridiculous charade.

When the young woman didn't back down and the villagers started shouting encouragement, he lost his temper. The gangster lunged for his Yongchun, grabbing at her hair, but his hand found nothing.

She rotated her torso, parried his outstretched arm, and slammed her palm into his jaw. In disbelief, his face stinging and red, he leaped forward again, throwing a furious right hook. Yongchun glided toward him, simultaneously blocking his strike with her forearm and thrusting her horizontal fist straight down the centerline into his nose.

With blood streaming down his face and his eyes watering, the thug came at her again. Yongchun turned as he swung so that she was always controlling the center space and his punches couldn't land. She responded with lightning-fast strikes, straight down the middle to his face, throat, and abdomen. Soon enough, the gangster's will to continue fighting broke, and he fled from the village in shame.

A few weeks later, Leung Bok Chau returned to the village, and she regaled him with her story as he listened in disbelief. It wasn't long before the couple married. Bok Chau dubbed her martial art "Yongchun Quan," or "Wing Chun's Fist," in her honor.

In the following years, the couple continued to develop and teach the system together. They passed their skills on to their fellow villagers, ensuring their safety. They also taught members of the "Red Junk Opera," a traveling troupe of performers whose ranks were comprised of many Ming loyalists and martial arts experts.

From the opera members, long quarterstaffs (boating poles) and butterfly swords were added to the system. Yongchun's tale caught the imagination of the masses, and coupled with Wing Chun's efficiency, it soon developed a strong following throughout southern China.

THE FACTS

In relation to the stories of Ng Mui and Yan Yongchun, there are several key issues which cast doubt on the early parts of the tale. While there are many styles of martial arts that are alleged to have developed from the Southern Shaolin Temple (several through Ng Mui herself), there has been an ongoing debate surrounding these claims.

Many scholars argue that there is a lack of historical evidence, such as Buddhist or governmental records, relating to the location and even the existence of the Southern Shaolin Temple. These factors coupled with stories about it that mirror those from "Northern Shaolin" also provide evidence that it only ever existed as myth.[3,4,5]

As previously discussed in relation to Bodhidharma's legend, we know the term "Shaolin" did not always apply to any specific location but was a generic term for various temples, particularly those associated with the Zen (Chan) Buddhist tradition. This would explain why, in different versions of the legend, the temple has been located variously in Henan, Fujian, and other regions.

Although many sources claim the Southern Shaolin Temple was burned down in the seventeenth century for harboring anti-Qing rebels and that Ng Mui was an elder who escaped, this tale also has little verifiable evidence.

The story has been recycled many times in works of both nonfiction and fiction, which are often contradictory. For example, in some versions of the story prior to the nineteenth century, Ng Mui was a conspirator who set the temple ablaze herself.[6]

It is also hard to ignore the striking similarities between the creation of Wing Chun by Ng Mui and that of Taijiquan by Zhang Sanfeng, who both allegedly drew inspiration from watching a crane battle a snake.

While it is not impossible that two separate, similar incidents occurred, the fact that other near-identical tales exist throughout the region makes coincidence seem less probable. For example, in the legends of Sumatran Silat, a woman watching a fight between a crane and a snake also appears as the catalyst for its inception.[7]

This specific incident appears to be a migratory legend, which was probably developed in one setting then retold and attributed to figures in other regions and among other peoples. However, the original source of the story is unknown.

It should also be recognized that "The Heaven and Earth Society" (a secretive, folk-religion sect, better known today as the "Triads"), also trace their lineage back to five elders who escaped the burning of the temple.

Much like Ng Mui, The Heaven, and Earth Society were anti-Qing rebels and are often tied historically to the development of Southern Chinese martial arts.[8] It is possible that early Wing Chun may have featured within their ranks as a quick-training, combative fighting style rather than being developed solely by Ng Mui and Yongchun.

For the duel itself, it appears unlikely that a young woman with minimal training and a large weight disadvantage could fend off a much larger, stronger, and more aggressive attacker with such ease. One only needs to look at the early days of mixed martial arts, when weight classes did not yet exist, to see the importance size plays in striking-based combat systems.

While Yongchun's defense may have been possible using certain highly effective techniques (e.g., throat, groin, or eye strikes), it seems probable that the emphasis of the "centerline theory"[9] and other typical techniques of Wing Chun are later incorporations to demonstrate the legitimacy of the system.

The latter parts of the legend in which the Red Junk Opera troupe are taught Wing Chun appear more credible, as from this point onwards, there is a traceable lineage. For example, the current surviving Grandmaster and son of Yip Man (Yip Ching), attributes his lineage to a Cantonese Opera performer named Ng Cheung who lived in the 1730s.[10]

It has also been suggested that the attribution of Wing Chun to female founders may have come from Ng Cheung specializing in playing female roles; or that it could have been inspired by some of the Hakka women who worked in silkworm factories around Canton and studied martial arts for self-defense.[11] If so, the name Yongchun/Wing Chun may have become associated with the style through an unknown female practitioner of this era.

In regard to modern Wing Chun's features, it could be argued that the conceptual practices of the style, (for example fighting with tight stances in small spaces) and the use of a nine-foot quarterstaff may be better suited to the boating communities and cramped city spaces of Canton rather than the temples and mountains inland.

Similarly, Wing Chun's dual butterfly knives are clearly more closely related to civilian items than military weapons. Judkins and Nielson note how such arms also formed the core weapons of nineteenth century militia training in the region.[12]

Finally, some scholars have also noted similarities to, and even suggested influence from, Western bare-knuckle boxing, pointing to features such as the low guard and focus on strikes to the torso with parallel fists, as well as protecting the body with low elbows.[13]

While these similarities may be purely coincidental, in the Cantonese port cities where Wing Chun gained popularity, many sailors of British and European descent did engage in martial contests with the locals. Therefore, it is within the realm of possibility that such practices may have been combined with other Chinese arts to create the modern Wing Chun practices we see today.

A young woman practices a Wing Chun butterfly knife form under the eaves of a temple, while her male peers observe.

Functions of the Legend

Inspiring Resistance or Rebellion

While there is little actual evidence to support Ng Mui's legend, or even the Southern Shaolin Temple's existence, there is considerable evidence that details Wing Chun's development within alternative communities or at a later time period. One possible reason for the popularity of the Ng Mui/Yongchun origin story is that it was originally part of an arsenal of resistance tales told among groups of the repressed throughout nineteenth and twentieth century China.

The narrative surrounding Ng Mui is explicitly unfavorable toward the ruling Qing Dynasty (against whom there were many rebellions from the middle of the nineteenth century until the early twentieth century). Therefore, the tale may have originally served a propaganda purpose, painting the Qing in a negative light and creating figureheads that rebels may aspire to emulate.

In particular, the "Heaven and Earth Society" or other groups may have used such stories as recruitment tools for their causes. After all, a good fighting-the-power story, in the right context, can be extremely powerful.

Regardless of whether Wing Chun was born out of the mystical Southern Shaolin Temple or among the boating communities of Canton, this type of story, in which an ordinary 'everyman' (or woman) stands up to their oppressors, has near-universal appeal. This appeal has no doubt contributed in some part to the widespread popularity of Wing Chun both historically and in the modern day.

Legitimizing Wing Chun Principles

As Wing Chun training usually focuses upon precision and proper form with a relatively small set of core techniques, the Ng Mui/Yan Yongchun legend emphasizes these elements, and in doing so "proves" their legitimacy by showing their effectiveness in combat.

Within the legend, we can clearly see a number of the core physical practices and techniques of the system. These include the centerline principle, the simultaneous strike, the parry (*Pak Sao*), and pivoting stances used to defend against side-on attacks (*Juen Ma*). All of these techniques are present in most mainstream Wing Chun systems today.

Furthermore, as Wing Chun (in the legend at least) was both developed and used with great success by women against stronger attackers, it emphasizes how a focus on speed and technique may be able to overcome pure muscular strength.

Another core principle of the system is demonstrated in Yongchun's training, which in most iterations of the story lasts less than a year. This emphasizes how the system was designed to be taught as a practical means of self-defense in a relatively short time, rather than as an ongoing spiritual awakening that may take years to master, distinguishing it from most "Northern Shaolin" counterparts and demonstrating it to be a southern in origin.

References & Figures

[1] Hennessy, J. (2011). *The Essence of Martial Arts: Making Your Skills Work in Practice*. iUniverse.

[2] Hennessy. (2011).

[3] Henning, S. (2018). "Southern Fists and Northern Legs: Geography of Chinese Boxing." In M. Demarco, ed., *Henning's Scholarly Works on Chinese Combative Traditions* (pp. 34–43). Via Media Publishing. pp. 34–35.

[4] Buckler, S. (2016) "Wing Chun Kuen: A Revised Historical Perspective (Part 1)." *IMAS Quarterly* 5 (4): pp. 22–37. ISSN 2049-3649.

[5] Buckler, S. (2017) "Wing Chun Kuen: A Revised Historical Perspective (Part 2: Red Junks, Pirates and Secret Societies)." *IMAS Quarterly* 6 (1), 32–56.

[6] Judkins, B. N., & Nielson, J. (2015). *The Creation of Wing Chun: A Social History of the Southern Chinese Martial Arts*. State University of New York Press. p. 9.

[7] Green, T. A. (2001). *Martial Arts of the World: An Encyclopedia*. ABC Clio. P525.

[8] Judkins & Nielson. (2015). p. 51.

[9] A strategy which protects and attacks the central line of the torso. This is said to provide speed by striking along the most direct path toward crucial targets.

[10] Judkins & Nielson. (2015). p. 61.

[11] Green. (2001). p. 674.

[12] Judkins & Nielson. (2015). p. 93.

[13] Godwin in Green. (2001). p. 783.

Page 61 photo is from the author's personal collection.

NAI KHANOMTOM
The Hero of Ayutthaya Fights for Freedom

Nai Khanom Tom was born in the kingdom of Ayutthaya in approximately 1767. Despite rumored ties to royalty, it is probable that he belonged to a peasant family.

Depictions of Nai Khanom Tom often show him as a typical Thai fighter, with a wiry frame and high muscle mass. He is virtually always adorned in the fight attire of Muay Boran (Traditional Muay Thai) with his hands wrapped in braided ropes that extend around the thumb and knuckles up to the wrist and forearms. Khanom Tom also wears a rope bandana (*Mongkhon*) and upper-arm wraps (*Pra Jiad*), both of which are donned by experienced fighters to indicate their skill level, similar to a black belt in Karate or Taekwondo.

As a soldier he likely learned Muay Boran and had military combat training, which probably included both unarmed and armed methods, as was customary in the Ayutthayan Kingdom.

Today Khanom Tom is recognized as the patriarch of modern Muay Thai and Muay Boran. He is also known for winning his freedom from the King of Burma (present-day Myanmar) on account of his fighting prowess.

During the eighteenth and nineteenth centuries, Nai Khanom Tom became a widely revered folk-hero in Thailand. Today, there are many statues and museums dedicated to him across the country. He is immortalized in comic books, TV shows, and movies, and is even revered annually on March seventeenth, which is "Nai Khanom Tom Day."

THE LEGEND

The battle had been bloody and brutal. Despite conscripting almost every young and healthy male in Ayutthaya, the Kingdom had eventually fallen to the overwhelming might of the Burmese King's army.

It was mid-1767 when the Burmese entered the once glorious metropolis of Ayutthaya, the namesake city of the kingdom. The victorious soldiers sacked the city and took every man that remained alive as a prisoner.

The Burmese King Mangra soon set about establishing order in the fallen capital. Rather than ruling with an iron fist, he was wise enough to know that he needed to win local support. In a bid to demonstrate that his people were not just fearsome warriors but also men of faith and fairness, the King decided to usher in his reign with a seven-day Buddhist festival.

Coming from a nation with strong martial traditions, and keen to see how his own men would stack up against the renowned boxers of Ayutthaya, the King decided to include martial arts contests in the festival. He ordered his men to find worthy challengers among the prisoners, and decreed that any fighter who could defeat his Burmese champion would earn their freedom.

King Mangra's troops worked through the makeshift prison barracks, looking for fighters, and one name kept coming up: Nai Khanom Tom. Rumor had it he was the best boxer in the city, a man who floated on air and whose fists cracked like lightning.

When the soldiers finally located Khanom Tom among the prisoners, he immediately volunteered, hoping to demonstrate that his people's fighting spirit could not be broken so easily.

As the opening day of the festival dawned, feasts, music, and dancing filled the streets. Burmese soldiers erected a square platform in the city center so that the display of the Burmese fighters' prowess would be seen by all. Workers then built a dais above it, adorned with a gilded throne that would allow King Mangra to preside over the spectacle.

* * *

It was mid-afternoon when the fights began. The first bouts went as expected, with the battle-hardened Burmese soldiers easily overpowering their already battered and malnourished prisoners.

When Khanom Tom's turn arrived, the guards led him into the makeshift arena. Rather than making his way straight to the center of the platform, the fighter worked his way around the edge of the space in a dance. He climbed up onto the platform and bowed at each corner in veneration of his teachers and the Gods (a tradition now known as *Wai Khru Ram Muay*).

Some of the Burmese took this act as an affront; the strange prisoner must have been trying to invoke some kind of curse or black magic against them. Why else perform the bizarre ritual?

The King watched, amused by the strange display. Then he glanced over at his first fighter, a powerful champion boxer from the rugged north of Burma, and was confident that victory was all but assured.

Khanom Tom finally met his opponent in the middle of the arena. If the raucous calls of spectators were anything to go by, they were expecting the Burmese champion to make short work of the weakened prisoner, even if he was one of Ayutthaya's best fighters.

The bout began. The two men circled for a few moments, then the Burmese champion advanced hard and fast. Khanom Tom kept out of punching range, smashing his opponent's legs repeatedly with his shins, which were hard as steel after years of kicking banana trees in training.

The Burmese fighter grew frustrated and dived in to cut off his opponent. Khanom Tom exploded back at him with a flurry of fists, elbows, and knees.

By the time the champion managed to retreat out of range, his arms and legs were battered from defending himself, making his footwork slow and his blocks even slower. Seeing his chance, Khanom Tom swung a high roundhouse kick up over his opponent's guard, slamming his shin into the Burmese fighter's temple and knocking him out cold.

The crowd erupted with anger, shouting accusations that the Ayutthayan had cheated with his black magic rituals. The referee stated that the fight was unfair, ruling that the dancing and sorcery had distracted Khanom Tom's opponent. The King rose from his throne, acknowledging the accusation, and ordered a second opponent to be brought in.

One by one, seven other Burmese fighters stepped up onto the platform. The first fell to a spinning heel kick to the head, the second Khanom Tom destroyed with knees to the torso from the clinch. During the third bout, the Ayutthayan slipped his opponent's punches and knocked him out with a fist to the jaw. Four more followed in quick succession.

Despite being allowed no time to rest between matches, having no support, and a crowd who were utterly against him, Khanom Tom prevailed, taking down one fighter after another.

Like the spectators, the fights outraged the King at first, but with each progressive win, he found himself growing in awe and respect for Khanom Tom's speed, power, and skill.

With eight fighters now dispatched, the King handed the Ayutthayan one final, impossible challenge. A second, renowned Burmese champion from the southwest of the country. He was a huge, bear-like fighter facing an exhausted opponent. Surely, he could not lose too?

The mountain of a man came out throwing everything he had at the Ayutthayan, but his legs were no match for the blasting low kicks he received in return. Finally, the big man caught hold of Khanom Tom, lifting him into a bear hug, but the smaller fighter slammed an elbow down onto the top of the champion's head. Like the eight before him, the Burmese fighter fell.

The King rose to his feet, not sure if he was more amazed or angered by Khanom Tom's victory and addressed the crowd. "This man fights as though he has venom on his hands; had the nobles fought like him, Ayutthaya would never have fallen."[1]

In recognition of the courage and iron will of Nai Khanom Tom, the King rewarded him with his freedom. For his defeat of the champions, gold and wives were gifted to the fighter.

Despite offers to join King Mangra's court and train his men, Khanom Tom left the occupied city and ventured into the highlands in the country's north.

Away from the watchful eye of the authorities, he taught his martial arts to thousands of students. They came from all over the country to learn from the man that briefly united their nation against the foreign invaders, proving once and for all that the Ayutthayan people were no easy conquest.

THE FACTS

The legend of Nai Khanom Tom's challenge is without doubt an inspiring story. It has been repeated countless times in various formats over the years, most notably in film, television, and as an oral tradition shared by Muay Thai and Muay Boran fighters.

The narrative itself is noticeably, a near-perfect rendition of a classic underdog story, in which the protagonist must fight for his way of life against a far more powerful, foreign threat. While this does not establish any further facts, it does suggest that the tale has likely been retold, reprinted, and exaggerated so many times that its historical reliability is extremely low.

While there is evidence that an incident somewhat reminiscent of Khanom Tom's legend took place, there are several known facts that can give further insight into its accuracy.

First, it should be highlighted that rather than stemming from Thai sources, the initial written account of the festival and Nai Khanom Tom's bouts comes from an eight-line Burmese poem. This was later popularized in a Thai-produced text called "Chronicles of Ayutthaya," compiled progressively throughout the seventeenth and eighteenth centuries.[2]

The first written version of the legend was brief and provided very few details about the actual fights. However the Burmese origin of the tale lends itself favorably to establishing that the story was at least grounded in reality. However, it is unlikely that the original version of events would have seen the contest in the Thai-positive light in which it is now told. In fact, some Burmese accounts written later state that Khanom Tom was a political prisoner who trained in *their* native martial arts, and that he was later released thanks to his pro-Burmese attitude rather than his fighting prowess.[3]

While Nai Khanom Tom is referred to in many texts as a common foot soldier, various Thai versions of the tale paint him as an aristocrat or member of royalty. Being of high social status would certainly be consistent with Khanom Tom being held as a political prisoner, however this claim may alternatively have begun as an attempt to create a royalist history for the Thai national sport.[4]

Conversely, the idea of Khanom Tom being a foot soldier is supported by the fact that there were government-led meetings held in recent years aimed at selecting a new figurehead for Muay Thai, with stronger royal connections.[5]

Returning to the commonly told version of the legend, while the number of foes defeated varies depending on the specific retelling, there is at least some chance that a skilled boxer may have been able to prevail against multiple opponents.

The Burmese military successes of the period relied heavily on weapon usage, for which they recruited and specifically trained many peasant villagers. Similarly, the Burmese were also known to be more skilled in wrestling than boxing traditions during this period.[6] These factors together show that a lack of unarmed pugilistic skills may have contributed to some of Khanom Tom's apparent successes.

In terms of the physical aspects of the legend, specifically the dance and "black magic," it is often claimed that Khanom

Tom performed the Wai Khru Ram Muay (a dance which is performed prior to Muay Thai fights to venerate teachers, ancestors, and the Buddha).

Although there is little verifiable evidence of this event besides recent retellings, there were certainly dances that featured within martial arts contests during the period.[7] As a result, Khanom Tom's use of something similar to Wai Khru Ram Muay is possible, even though the performance itself may have varied significantly from the type seen in modern Muay Thai.

Another physical feature of the Thai-constructed legend is the account of specific techniques used by Khanom Tom during his fights. These details of the tale were certainly not present in earlier tellings, and have been gradually added and embellished upon over time.

For example, there is no clear evidence that pre-modern Thai fighters would have used spinning heel kicks at all.[8] In fact, it is doubtful a trained soldier during a period of conflict would have deliberately practiced a technique that would leave his back exposed during armed battles, or that he would have even engaged in hand-to-hand combat unless faced with no other option.

A fighter performs the Wai Khru Ram Muay before a modern kickboxing bout in Thailand.

FUNCTIONS OF THE LEGEND

Nationalist Development

Although there is reasonable evidence to suggest that Nai Khanom Tom's legend stems from fact, it is not a coincidence that the modern version of the tale first appeared when anti-Burmese sentiments were running high during the late eighteenth and early-nineteenth centuries. It then came to widespread popularity during the twentieth century, when Thailand was striving to create a unique national identity.[9]

By emphasizing a common enemy in the Burmese, who have often been seen historically as a rival (or even outright enemy of both Thailand and Buddhism), the legend promotes a clear sense of Thai nationalism.

Through both his fighting ability and spirit, the tale implies that Khanom Tom's skills are something both uniquely Thai and that they (and consequently their practitioners) are superior when compared to Burmese Bando and other Southeast Asian kickboxing styles. As one scholar states, "It was in this way that Muay Thai became a brick in the nationalist myth."[10]

Creating a Military Background for Muay Thai

Nai Khanom Tom's legend creates a traceable lineage for Muay Thai to warriors from ancient times (and also manages to include royalist elements). While the link to ancient battlefield techniques is spurious at best, it has served as a valuable tool for the propagation of Muay Thai and Muay Boran both locally and internationally.

Modern Muay Thai is often represented as an ancient Ayutthayan battlefield system, rather than as a long-standing combat sport, which has almost identical iterations in countries across Southeast Asia.

By tying specific techniques to Khanom Tom (and by association, the military), historical links have been forged that provide perceived authenticity for their existence and use within modern Muay Thai. After all, if it was good enough for a soldier in a fight to the death, it should be good enough for us!

From my own experiences studying both Muay Thai in Thailand and other Southeast Asian kickboxing systems, it is clear that centuries of ongoing refinement within an often intense and brutal combat arena have created a highly nuanced and efficient martial art. One which I would argue is more practical and relevant for modern-day practitioners than hypothetical methods for engaging enemies with swords, spears, or bows in combat.

Legitimizing Modern-Day Techniques

Elements of Khanom Tom's legend, such as the Wai Khru Ram Muay and the specific strikes used in his bouts, provide us with further evidence that Muay Thai's background was predominantly sporting. However, their placement into legends like this helps to create a distinctively Thai arsenal of techniques that appear in modern Muay Thai and Muay Boran (even though most of them also exist in numerous other systems).

Regardless of whether such events actually took place and how they unfolded, the legend has served valuable functions in creating part of the Thai national identity. It has provided practitioners of Muay Thai with direct links from historical warriors to their current practices, and helped turn Muay Thai from a peasant sport into a source of national pride, imbued with patriotic and heroic ideals.

References & Figures

[1] Vail, P. T. (1998). Modern Muay Thai Mythology. *Crossroads: An Interdisciplinary Journal of Southeast Asian Studies* 12(2): 75–95. p. 80.

[2] Vail (1998).

[3] Green, T. A. (2001). *Martial Arts of the World: An Encyclopedia.* ABC Clio. p. 631.

[4] Vail, P. T. (2014). Muay Thai: Inventing Tradition for a National Symbol. *Journal of Social Issues in Southeast Asia* 29(3): 509–553. https://doi.org/10.1355/sj29-3a. p. 549.

[5] Vail. (2014). p. 515.

[6] Green. (2001). p. 814.

[7] Louber, D. L. (1693). *A New Historical Relation of the Kingdom of Siam.* Horne. p. 49.

[8] Vail. (1998). p. 81.

[9] Monthienvichienchai , A. (2004). "The Changes in the Role and Significance of Muay Thai, 1920-2003." (Thesis.) Chulalongkorn University, Bangkok. p. 43.

[10] Monthienvichienchai, A. (2004).

Page 72 photo: Kru Tony Moore, CC BY-SA 4.0 <https://creativecommons.org/licenses/by-sa/4.0>, via Wikimedia Commons

CHOI HONG-HI
Leading Korea from the Ashes of War

Choi Hong-Hi was born on November 9th, 1918, in the Myongchon Province, the northernmost region of what is now part of the Democratic People's Republic of Korea (North Korea).

He is said to have trained in Taekkyeon (a historical Korean kicking martial art and game, somewhat similar to modern-day Capoeira) under Han Il Dong. He also studied Shotokan Karate in Japan under Gichin Funakoshi, up to second-degree black belt.

Choi Hong-Hi was famously small in stature but also a stern and serious figure who seemed to embody the stoic principles of military martial arts. Almost every photo of Hong-Hi shows him in formal attire, be it a suit, Taekwondo *Dobok*, or full military uniform.

After being exiled from South Korea for political reasons (due in part to working with North Korea to establish Taekwondo), Hong-Hi eventually returned to the north, where he lived until his death on June fifteenth, 2002.

Choi Hong-Hi is now known as the founder and grandmaster of ITF Taekwondo, and his distinctions include second-degree Shotokan black belt, general of the Korean army, and veteran of the Japanese military.

Modern Taekwondo is typically represented by two schools, World Taekwondo (WT) and the International Taekwondo Federation (ITF). The ITF identifies Choi Hong-Hi as their founder and the patriarch of Taekwondo. The WT considers him an important figure, but not ultimately responsible for the development of the modern sport. The association and later disassociation of Hong-Hi with Taekwondo lineages is complex yet of great interest to both parties alike.

This legend has been considered as a Rebellion Tale due to its overarching theme and message of fighting against the Japanese occupation, and later developing a martial art seen as being uniquely Korean.

THE LEGEND

With his eyes fixed on the dank and moldy walls of his cell, Choi Hong-Hi wondered if he'd made a terrible mistake.

Just a few weeks before, he'd been a soldier, a martial artist, and a patriot. Now, locked in a cell awaiting an indefinite trial date that never seemed to come, he was nothing. The trial would either assign him to the cells for the rest of his days, or the more likely option, end with him facing the firing squad.

For over thirty years, the Japanese armies had dominated his homeland, plunging the Korean people into poverty and famine. Someone had to fight back, and that was exactly what Hong-Hi and twenty-nine other young soldiers had done. Together they had founded the "Pyongyang Student Soldiers' Movement" with plans to rebel, kill their commanders, and escape to join Kim Il Sung's anti-Japanese movement to the north. However, when a spy in their midst betrayed the group, the occupying rulers of the country came down on Hong-Hi and his team of rebels like a thundering tsunami.

As the days turned to weeks and the weeks to months, Hong-Hi focused on the only thing that could keep his mind occupied and his spirit strong through this seemingly endless purgatory: martial arts.

There was a problem with this, though. The space of his cramped cell made it difficult for Hong-Hi to work through his usual Shotokan Karate kata as he would in an open space. He found his long strikes, especially his kicks, cut short by the cell walls.

Not wanting to lose the power and speed he had spent so long developing, Hong-Hi worked on extending his kicks higher instead, snapping his feet out and pulling them back fast like they would do in Taekkyeon. It was here that the first foundations of what would eventually become Taekwondo were born.

It was a wintry morning in 1944 when one of the regular guards passed Hong-Hi's cell. He was a Japanese jailer, but this one was slightly more lenient and less likely to dole out beatings than his counterparts.

Through a mixture of Japanese and broken Korean, the guard inquired curiously about what his captive was practicing, seeing that it looked different from his own Japanese martial arts. Noticing the jailer obviously had an interest in the martial arts, Hong-Hi replied, telling him it was a mix of Taekkyeon and Karate.

Even though he knew it was risky, Hong-Hi took a gamble and asked the guard if he could train somewhere outside of his cell. The jailer smiled. He told the prisoner that he would let him train in the courtyard, but only if he would share some of his techniques. This sounded immediately suspect. Was there going to be some kind of punishment for the audacity of his request?

In the gray morning light of the courtyard, the guard asked Hong-Hi to repeat his techniques while he and two of his colleagues looked on. Apprehensive, the Korean worked through his form of Shotokan Karate, snapping his kicks high and powerful as his Taekkyeon training had taught him.

After a few minutes, the guards fell in behind, trying to mirror the prisoner's movements. Practicing alone was one thing, but teaching the Japanese guards their country's own system of martial arts seemed like a recipe for disaster. Surely someone would take offense.

Much to Hong-Hi's surprise, the guards called on him to deliver these sessions frequently. Each time, more staff and prisoners came to train with him. Eventually, he was even allowed to create a makeshift dojo in the prison gymnasium.

For the best part of the following year, Hong-Hi's training and teaching once again gave him something to live for, but that was all about to change for the worse.

After a seemingly endless wait, the Japanese finally dragged Hong-Hi before a judge to be tried for his crimes. By some stroke of luck he avoided the death sentence, and the judge handed him a seven-year incarceration in its place. The would-be instigator of rebellion was then transferred from the holding jail to Pyongyang central prison.

The conditions in the North Korean facility were hideous. Hong-Hi shared his cell with half a dozen men, all of whom were suffering from malnourishment, injury, and leper-like skin diseases after being constantly beaten, starved, and deprived of basic hygiene by their guards.

Soon Hong-Hi grew weak and sick too; any hopes of freedom or life beyond his cell now seemed like distant dreams. The young rebel was now certain that by the time death came for him, he would welcome the relief.

Fortunately for Hong-Hi, just a few months into his incarceration the American nuclear strikes on Hiroshima and Nagasaki seemed to do the impossible and abruptly ended Japanese domination of the Pacific region. Japan surrendered unconditionally to the USA, relinquishing their Korean colonies in the process.

On the morning of the surrender, most of the Japanese prison guards fled and left their Korean subordinates in charge. Hong-Hi and many of his peers, most of whom were political prisoners, were released in the turmoil.

Had the Korean guards taken pity on them? Had they just stopped caring? Either way, Hong-Hi and his colleagues quickly made a break for freedom before another party could reinstate control.

* * *

After his escape, Hong-Hi journeyed south to Seoul, where he enlisted in the newly formed Korean military. It didn't take long for his skills in martial arts and his experience leading Korean independence movements to gain him a promotion to lieutenant. This position gave him a springboard from which to launch his new system, then named Tang Soo Do.

As he rose through the ranks, eventually up to general, Hong-Hi further refined his martial art all the while searching for suitable candidates to help him develop the system further. One of these came in the form of a military expert and renowned martial artist named Nam Tae-Hi.

Hong-Hi had learned that during a previous battle, Tae-Hi

had been stranded on a mountaintop watchpost when it was attacked in a night raid by the Chinese communists.

After losing his weapon, Tae-Hi had engaged in a brutal hand-to-hand combat in the dugout trenches on the hillside for over ten hours. Throughout the night, the young soldier killed more than twenty men with nothing but his fists and feet. If there was anyone who had the combat knowledge to help Hong-Hi develop and promote his system, Tae-Hi was that man.

In 1955, a panel of military advisors, martial arts masters, and historians met to unify the various styles of Korean martial arts under the umbrella of Hong-Hi's newly created system. With the general at the helm and his supporters at his side, the council decided on the name *Tae Kwon Do,* meaning *"the way of fists and feet."*

THE FACTS

Choi Hong-Hi and other leaders of what would later become known as "The Pyongyang Incident" were held for extended periods of time under Japanese orders. There are also several firsthand accounts confirming that Hong-Hi ended up teaching many of the prisoners and guards martial arts, and that they transformed part of the detention center into a gymnasium.[1]

While Hong-Hi claimed that he worked on developing (and teaching) a mix of Karate and Taekkyeon during his incarceration and the surrounding years, he later retracted his own words in a remarkably damning interview.

Hong-Hi stated: "There was nothing to Taekkyeon. Nothing more than a few of these kinds of foot moves" (he then demonstrated a couple of simple kicking motions).[2]

In the same interview, Hong-Hi also discussed how any attempts in the early days to link his martial arts practices to Taekkyeon would have ended up in rebellion from his students. He also identified how the lineage of Japanese Karate was the only aspect that gave their training legitimacy with respect to the martial arts.[3]

This casts doubt on both Taekkyeon being an inspiration for Taekwondo, but also upon the historical use of the system as a martial art entirely. Some scholars have even gone as far to suggest that the modern incarnation of Taekkyeon developed because of Taekwondo's popularity rather than vice versa, and that it was essentially reborn from its imagined use.[4] Techniques such as jumping back kicks, which were later adapted from Taekwondo back into the modern practice of Taekkyeon,[5] provide further evidence for this conclusion.

The training Hong-Hi had supposedly undertaken in Shotokan prior to his imprisonment is also dubious. At the time, there was only one Korean in Japan recorded to have been promoted to the level of second-degree black belt.[6]

As a foreigner training in the country, it is highly doubtful that Hong-Hi would have been able to reach this rank in only five years, let alone the two which he claims. The theory that he may have embellished his own training is supported by the testimonial of Nam Tae-Hi, who stated that he rarely saw Hong-Hi practice martial arts at all.[7]

Tae-Hi however, was highly skilled and also came from a Shotokan background. Although the only records discussing his use of fighting skills for self-defense in the military are from his own interviews and recollection, leaving them ultimately unverified. Tae-Hi's ongoing push for Taekwondo to be recognized as an efficient, practical system rather than a sport, lends his tale some credibility.[8]

While Hong-Hi obviously went through great hardships and found solace and pride in his training in martial arts, most tales of his skills as a fighter are relatively unfounded. Some suggest he was not even a particularly competent martial artist, and was promoted to an honorary fourth-degree black belt only due to his military position.[9] From my own experiences in Taekwondo and research conducted in writing this book, this seems plausible.[10]

As a result of the above, it may be worth considering that other key figures of Taekwondo's development (such as Nam Tae-Hi) are equally, if not more, deserving of the reverence bestowed upon Hong-Hi for their contributions to the system.

When naming the system, it is clear that Hong-Hi used the term Taekwondo in a linguistic attempt to further the idea of it being an indigenous Korean martial art (i.e., Taekkyeon) and probably utilized the typically Japanese suffix "Do" to make the system comparable to Japanese styles of Karate-Do, Kendo, Judo, and others. Regardless of this, most scholars concur that the naming of Taekwondo was one of several steps taken to invent a tradition that could be seen as being independent from its Japanese predecessors, despite virtually zero physical differences (in the early days at least).[11]

As Hong-Hi's claims of his early Taekkyeon influences became better known, tenuous historical ties were then pulled up to link the system to ancient Korean peoples and practices (such as the *Hwarang*, an alleged warrior class, who in reality were teenage aristocrats who performed songs, dances, and shamanism).[12]

Finally, spinning and flying kicks—which were likely not practiced by Hong-Hi during the period—were also later incorporated into the system on his instruction.[13] Although the reasons for these inclusions are purely speculative, it is likely that they were threefold. First, they served the purpose of impressing observers of the new martial art; second, they assisted in further differentiating Taekwondo from its Karate origins; and finally, they provided yet more "evidence" of Taekwondo's ancient links with Taekkyeon.

FUNCTIONS OF THE LEGEND

Nationalist Development

Hong-Hi is often considered as a man of grand vision who revived Korea's martial arts by incorporating ancient indigenous systems with modern Japanese styles. Unfortunately, for the latter part at least, this is most likely not the case.

However, Hong-Hi's tale, particularly that of his initial training and incorporation of Taekkyeon into modern Tae Kwon Do, serves several important functions for modern-day practitioners.

First, it allows us to practice a martial art that is clearly different from Japanese Karate by providing us a legitimate (or a least semi-plausible) rationale for the acrobatic and high-kicking techniques of Taekwondo that have become such a well-known part of the system.

While the historical grounding for these types of techniques are inaccurate, they continue to be propagated. For example, it is often claimed that Taekwondo's flying kicks come from trying to kick enemy attackers from horseback. However, as one scholar puts it, "You only have to have seen a horse, never mind someone sitting on it, never mind a warrior on a war-horse, to realize that this idea is ridiculous."[14]

This thought aside, as someone who has trained for a number of years in Taekwondo and thoroughly enjoyed the acrobatic

The "Dae Kwae Do" painted in 1846 appears to show both
Korean folk wrestling (above) and Taekkyeon (below).

elements of the system, I would argue that the use of these historical inaccuracies to develop a unique national martial art that is recognized across the globe is (somewhat) justified.

Creating a Rationale for Sportification

As the competitive elements of Taekwondo have been emphasized in recent years, even to the extent that Olympic competitors are referred to as "players," there has been a push for legitimization in the practice as a sport. This is a shift that is more easily accepted when considering the (alleged) roots of the system in an ancient kicking game.

While the modern sport's development has undoubtedly come at the expense of martial efficacy (and remains a controversial issue for many practitioners), to this author at least, the positive outcomes appear to far outweigh the negative. These include improved health, fitness, discipline, and mental focus for an estimated twenty million practitioners worldwide.[15] Many of these practitioners are likely aware of the gamification of the style, but are simply not bothered that martial efficacy takes a backseat in comparison to the sporting, tournament, and self-mastery aspects of Taekwondo.

Creating a Figurehead for Taekwondo

Regardless of his skills, Hong-Hi was undoubtedly an excellent figurehead for Taekwondo. As a general and a former Korean independence fighter, who was supported by martial artists of incredible talent, he managed to ride the wave of nationalism that followed decades of oppression at the hands of the Japanese.

Largely thanks to the credibility Hong-Hi earned from his time in prison camps and his military background, he was positioned to develop a system of "indigenous" Korean martial arts.

Early Taekwondo was also exceptionally marketed and promoted, even though it was essentially an invented tradition.

Through legends such as those related in this chapter, by incorporating aspects of Korean history into the names of the forms and including high kicks and the game-like approaches of Taekkyeon, Hong-Hi and his people *did* truly create a unique Korean martial art—just not one with the ancient links that he claimed!

A member of the "Korean Tigers" display team performs one of their signature high-flying kicks. Their silk uniforms are also reminiscent of modern Taekkyeon attire.

References & Figures

[1] Gillis, A. (2016). *A Killing Art: The Untold History of Tae Kwon Do*. ECW Press. p.31

[2] Taken from an interview with Choi in 2001. See Capener, S. (2016). "The Making of a Modern Myth: Inventing a Tradition for Taekwondo." *Korea Journal* 56(1): 61–92. https://doi.org/10.25024/kj.2016.56.1.61 p. 69.

[3] Capener (2016).

[4] Cho, S., Moenig, U., and Nam, D. (2012). "The Available Evidence Regarding T'AEKKYŎN and Its Portrayal as a 'Traditional Korean Martial Art.'" *Acta Koreana* 15(2): 341–368. https://doi.org/10.18399/acta.2012.15.2.004.

[5] Capener. (2016). p. 69.

[6] *International Taekwondo Federation*. General Choi Hong-Hi–International Taekwondo Federation. (n.d.). Retrieved November 25, 2021, from https://www.itf-tkd.org/general-choi-hong-hi/. p. 2.

[7] Gillis. (2016). p. 27.

[8] Gillis. (2016). p. 45.

[9] Moenig, U. (2013). "The Influence of Korean Nationalism on the Formational Process of Taekwŏndo in South Korea." *Archiv Orientalni*. p. 334.

[10] During research for this book I was unable to find any footage of Choi performing a solid/powerful technique. This is a suspicious absence given the quantity of Taekwondo demonstrations and seminars he led over the years.

[11] Bowman, P. (2016). "Making Martial Arts History Matter." *The International Journal of the History of Sport* 33(9): 915–933. https://doi.org/10.1080/09523367.2016.1212842. p. 3.

[12] Capener. (2016). p. 75.

[13] Gillis. (2016). p. 70.

[14] Bowman, P. (2017). *Mythologies of Martial Arts*. Rowman and Littlefield International. p. 55.

[15] Green, T. A. (2001). *Martial Arts of the World: An Encyclopedia*. ABC Clio. p. 611.

The image on page 85 is public domain.

Part III

DUELS

While possibly considered less heroic than leading a spiritual revolution, or standing up to a stronger invading force, the tales of duels within the canon of martial arts legends remain extremely important.

In particular, these tales often match a legendary figure or martial arts founder against a worthy opponent in a conflict that often acts as a catalyst for the development of their own unique style or skills. Similarly, many of these legends also offer rationale and justification for particular strategies or techniques used within each style, thus serving as both a historical tale and a modern-day teaching tool.

This section will therefore focus on the famous bouts of one person against another, as opposed to larger battles or challenges from other sources.

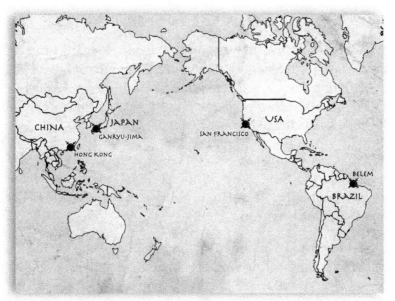

Key sites from Chapter Three: Ganryujima Island (Japan), Hong Kong, San Francisco (USA), and Belem (Brazil).

MIYAMOTO MUSASHI
A Swordsman Meets His Greatest Foe

Miyamoto Musashi was born as Miyamoto Bennosuke on March 1, 1584, in a southwestern province of Japan. His family came from a respected line of Samurai, and many of them were martial arts experts. This meant he could later take the high-status name Musashi.

Due to a period of war, he was taken in at a young age by his uncle, who was a Zen Buddhist monk and swordsman. He then trained in Kenjutsu, Bojutsu, and various schools of Japanese swordsmanship.

Musashi is usually pictured as a man of large stature for his time and location (this supports his famed skill of wielding two swords simultaneously). In many paintings, he has long hair tied up in a Samurai topknot, but his self-portraits later in life show him with thinning, shorter hair.

He is often pictured with a long mustache, bearded, and wearing a Kimono, all of which were popular styles with the sixteenth century Samurai.

Musashi died from what is now presumed to have been lung cancer on the thirteenth of June 1645, near Kumamoto on the southernmost main island of Japan. He is reported to have completed his masterwork, *The Book of Five Rings*, just three months before his death.

Musashi was one of the most feared and accomplished swordsmen in Japanese history and founder of the *Niten Ichi-Ryū* School. Besides this, he was a renowned painter, poet, and philosopher. Musashi's *The Book of Five Rings* remains among the most popular texts on martial arts strategy ever written.

While there is a lot of documentation surrounding Miyamoto Musashi, he has been portrayed in hundreds (if not thousands) of semi-fictional iterations in Japan and worldwide. Most notably in Eiji Yoshikawa's 1930s novelization of his life. This has led to some confusion over certain events of Musashi's legend, which, whether fictionalized or not, are truly astounding.

THE LEGEND

A heavy-handed bang on the front door echoed through the thin wooden walls of the merchant's house and jerked Musashi from a deep slumber. Warm rays were trailing in through the windows, letting him know that the sun was already high in the sky. Somewhere nearby, a flock of gulls squawked and shouted as they fought over the remains of the morning's catch.

The swordsman gazed up at the blue sky that hung over the port town, wondering what fate would await him today on the shore of the tiny island. Just then, the door to the guest room slid open and the head of the household entered, giving Musashi a nervous smile. His friend, Tarozaemon, told him that a messenger had arrived from Lord Hosokawa; the region's ruler had summoned him to depart at once.

It was already the hour of the dragon, and Musashi was late. Tarozaemon had a look of genuine concern in his eyes. The swordsman gave his friend a warm, reassuring smile and rose from the soft futon to his feet as if he had not a care in the world.

Today was the thirteenth of April, 1612, but the buildup to this duel had gone on for the best part of a year. When Musashi had taken up residence at a Zen temple in the ancient capital city of Kyoto, he'd met a vassal of a powerful southern lord named Hosokawa Tadaoki and eventually traveled south himself.

It was there that he had been introduced to Hosokawa's master of swords, the self-proclaimed greatest swordsman in Japan, nicknamed "The Demon of the Western Provinces." This man was Sasaki Kojiro.

Musashi had been traveling the country, studying the way of the sword and taking on challengers for more than a decade already, so he was not easily intimidated. His dueling days had begun when he was just thirteen years of age. Often, he found his thoughts returning to that first opponent, an arrogant young man who had refused to yield and paid for it with his life.

Thirty or more duels later, Musashi remained undefeated. He had built a reputation as a fearsome fighter, uninterested in the rules and politics of the Samurai, caring only for the way of the sword itself. As a result, he had only taken on a handful of disciples. Most were simply not committed enough to follow their renegade master as he crossed the length and breadth of Japan to prove he was the best there had ever been.

Naturally, soon after he ventured south, an explosive rivalry developed between him and Kojiro. The two swordsmen could hardly have been cut from more different cloth. Musashi was a wandering vagabond who fought on instinct, strength of will, and with reckless abandon, while Kojiro was a technical master, known for his legendary speed and accuracy. His use of an extra-long sword nicknamed "The Drying Pole" emphasized these strengths even further.

Musashi was a warrior born and raised, and when Kojiro disrespected him by publicly claiming his skills were superior and that Musashi was nothing more than a thug, he could not abide the insult to his honor. Soon after, he petitioned Lord Hosokawa, asking him to grant them permission for a martial arts challenge. Either he would emerge victorious, truly the best swordsman in the land, or he would die with honor, his life taken in glorious combat.

The provincial ruler had agreed, providing the setting for the duel on a tiny, isolated island. Musashi had wondered whether this was simply a tactic to protect Kojiro's honor if he should lose. Either way, the rivalry between him and Lord Hosokawa's retainer had reached a boiling point. Today, one man would live and become a legend, the other would die.

Slowly, Musashi dressed. He fastened a kimono around his waist with a silk belt and wrapped a bandana around his head. He washed his face and ate a leisurely breakfast. Only when a second messenger arrived, fearing he had fled, did Musashi agree to leave. Tarozaemon wished his friend luck and sent one of his servants to row him to the island from the nearby docks.

"Thank you for your help my friend," Musashi said, "but may I ask one more favor? Can I borrow an oar?"[1]

Tarozaemon didn't understand. He'd already provided men to row the boat, and what could Musashi do to help with a single oar? Regardless, he obliged.

* * *

It was the hour of the serpent when Musashi's tiny rowboat pulled into the shallows of Ganryujima Island; more than two hours after the agreed-upon time. Out in the open ocean, the rough waves had rocked the small fishing vessel wickedly, while in the bay all was calm and still. Throughout the trip, Musashi had kept his focus on the borrowed oar, whittling it down with his short sword until it was the perfect size and shape.

Watching the boat drift casually into the bay from where he stood under the hot mid-morning sun, Kojiro drew "The Drying Pole," itching for it to taste his enemy's blood.

Deftly, Musashi sprang from the boat and strode through the ankle-deep tide, holding the wooden sword he had carved from Tarozaemon's oar low by his side.

"I got here early. Why are you so late? Did you get scared?" Kojiro demanded.[2]

Musashi ignored the question and continued to stride through the shallows.

That is when Kojiro noticed the carved wooden sword in his hands. *Does he really intend to face me with that?!* Kojiro wondered, his face twisted in contempt. Showing up hours late armed with only a piece of wood was an insult too great for him to bear. In anger, Kojiro drew his sword and made a show of throwing his scabbard into the shallows.

"You've already lost," Musashi called over the sound of the wind and surf. "Would a man who expected to win throw away his scabbard?"[3]

Part III: Duels

Overwhelmed by fury, Kojiro charged.

Ten feet from his opponent, "The Demon of the Western Provinces" raised his sword high. As they came within range, Kojiro ripped his strike down with terrifying force, aiming to cleave his enemy's head in two.

Musashi answered with a horizontal swing of his own. In an instant, "The Drying Pole" slashed down in front of Musashi's eyes. He twisted his torso at the last second. Kojiro's cut came so close it cut the knot of the bandana from his head.

The ankle-deep water had slowed both of their steps and in doing so may have saved Musashi's life. Kojiro's eyes widened with horror as he realized that the strike had fallen short. An instant later, Musashi's wooden sword thundered into the side of his head with a sickening thud. Kojiro's knees buckled, his eyes rolled, and he dropped into the shallow waters.

Just as "The Demon of the Western Provinces" had famously shown no mercy to his rivals, Musashi offered him the same and slammed the heavy oar down onto his chest, killing him instantly.

The officials assigned to watch the match stood in silent awe as Musashi marched back to Tarozaemon's boat, jumped nimbly aboard, and started rowing out of the bay. Kojiro's pride had been his downfall and Musashi's legacy was assured.

THE FACTS

While most tellings of Musashi's legend focus on his clash with Kojiro, there are many others that document duels during his lifetime. One notable bout comes from his youth. At age thirteen Musashi fought against Arima Kihei, another arrogant young swordsman from the Shinto-Ryu school, who he quickly killed.[4]

Statues of Musashi and Kojiro battling upon the shore of
Ganryujima Island.

Musashi states in *The Book of Five Rings*, a treatise on life and
the way of the warrior that was his magnum opus, that "I
dueled more than sixty times, never once did I lose, that all
took place between the time I was thirteen years old and the
time I was twenty-nine."[5]

During this time, Musashi developed the dual-sword fighting
techniques that cemented his reputation as one of the greatest
martial artists of his day; he created the "Nitten-Ichi-Ryu"
(The School of Two Heavens as One), and wrote extensively
on swordsmanship.

While the specific number of Musashi's duels is difficult to
verify, many of them are documented in local family records
throughout Japan. Therefore, historians concur the quantity is
likely to be close to sixty if not more, as well as his involvement
in various military campaigns.[6]

However, there is some confusion in this case, as several events
of Musashi's life have been influenced by fiction. For example,
it is often stated that he was on the losing side of the Battle

of Sekigahara (which was one of the most decisive battles in Japanese history); however, records show that during that period he was supporting his father on a campaign on Japan's southern island.[7]

This creative interpretation of such events seems to have begun with the writing of Yoshikawa Eiji in his classic work based on the life of the swordsman[8] and may only have served as a plot device to create an interesting story.

In relation to the legendary duel, most accounts are said to stem from the *Nitenki,* a collection of stories about Musashi and his followers that was penned in 1755.[9]

However, there are controversies surrounding the Nitenki account. First, Musashi and Kojiro were almost certainly aware of each other's reputations, and some level of rivalry may have existed between the two (as they were both essentially contenders for the same accolade). Some scholars, however, believe that they had probably not met in person before the morning of the fight.

A letter sent by Musashi to Matsui Okinaga, who had trained under his father and acted as a messenger between him and Lord Hosokawa, supports the idea that they were strangers. The letter read, "It would seem as though a Ganryu Sasaki Kojiro is now residing in this area, and I have heard that his technique is excellent. My request is for permission for us to have a 'comparison of techniques.'"[10]

The motivations for organizing the fight on the tiny, isolated island are unknown, but it is plausible that Lord Hosokawa did want to avoid shame if his sword master was defeated. Another explanation may be for the Lord to absolve himself of any ramifications of a public battle, since both swordsmen had sizable followings. This might explain why he also prohibited all public observations of the clash.

 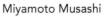

There are also disagreements about the age of Kojiro at the time of the duel. Because of contradictory statements in accounts, some historians argue he was still a teenager and therefore Musashi was his senior in both age and dueling experience while others claim Kojiro was at least fifty years old, due to certain professional accomplishments in his lifetime.

Various records, including his own works, state that Musashi was in his late twenties when the duel took place. If Kojiro was significantly older or younger, his opponent would have had a huge physical advantage. It is unlikely that Lord Hosokawa would have condoned such a duel, and therefore it is probable they were of a similar age.

While it is often assumed that Musashi's late and unarmed arrival at the duel was merely a show of bravado or nonchalance, there is a convincing argument that this was part of a threefold strategy on the part of the swordsman. Common themes throughout his written works include creating opportunities through throwing off opponents' equilibrium, creating physical advantages, and the use of surprise and fear to gain the upper hand in battle.[11]

By arriving late and making Kojiro wait in the scorching sun, growing evermore impatient and frustrated, Musashi would have given himself a strong psychological advantage.

By fashioning his wooden sword from an oar, Musashi may have mitigated his enemy's physical advantages of speed and reach by providing himself with a longer weapon—possibly just an inch or so longer than Kojiro's infamous "Drying Pole."

Disembarking in the shallows may have also allowed Musashi to disguise the length of his weapon, giving him the advantage of surprise.

Finally, while most records of the duel are favorable towards Musashi, there are also accounts (such as that of Harada Mukashi, who was in attendance) that tell a different tale.

He states how both fighters arrived at a similar time and Musashi did not kill Kojiro outright, but that after being knocked down he was beaten to death by his enemy's followers who had hidden on the island. Then, after using "dishonorable" tricks to achieve victory, Musashi allegedly fled the scene to save himself from repercussions.[12]

This version of events is not without evidence. For example, the island itself was not named Ganryujima until years after the duel took place. As Ganryu is Kojiro's lineage name (with "jima" meaning island), it seems likely that if Musashi's victory had been decisive and honorable, the island would have been named in his honor rather than after his defeated adversary.

If true, it may not have been Musashi's intention for Kojiro to die at all. After knocking him down, it would have been easy enough to deliver a final *coup de grâce* to his enemy, relatively repercussion free. But Musashi later told how they were not "true enemies" and that their match was merely a "comparison of techniques."[13]

Regardless, in most modern incarnations, Kojiro is painted as an arrogant villainous character. Some historians hypothesize that this idea came into popularity as the battle became a common scene for plays during the Edo period (1603 to 1867). This idea of Kojiro's villainy was then cemented further by Eiji Yoshikawa, who chose to portray him as the main antagonist in his 1930s semi-fictional novel *Musashi*.

It is clear that the rivalry between Musashi and Kojiro has been exaggerated for dramatic effect, with the former cast as an archetypal hero and the latter as the villain.

In the eyes of some, Musashi's tactics may have been cowardly or dishonorable, while for others, they may have just been prerequisites for his own survival.

Finally though, we know for certain that the duel *did* take place, and kudos must go to the fact that Musashi *did* triumph against one of Japan's greatest swordsmen, sporting only a piece of wood!

FUNCTIONS OF THE LEGEND

Creating a Figurehead for *Budō*

Although the legend of Musashi and Kojiro has been told for centuries by word of mouth, in plays, books, newspapers, movies, and TV, the veracity of the tale (as it is commonly recycled at least) is questionable. However, it remains an important part of the Japanese martial arts canon for a number of reasons, particularly in relation to the concept of Budo, which is the Japanese term meaning "The Way of the Warrior." In modern times, Budo incorporates not just martial arts practices, but serves as a combined code of conduct, philosophy, and spirituality.

It is well known that several semi-fictional plays, stories, and books, such as Eiji Yoshikawa's seminal work, helped transform the popular image of the swordsman "from that of a brutal killer into one of an enlightened master of self-cultivation."[14]

As we know, history is written by the winners, and while the unsavory aspects of Musashi's legend are often brushed over, it is likely that he was not simply the heroic philosopher swordsman portrayed today, but rather a complex human being who took lives in cold blood, but also completed works of great merit.

While Musashi's track record of duels to the death seems to support the latter representation, it should be recognized that in his later years, he did appear to veer more towards a peaceful philosophy, embracing Buddhist principles and the arts. Even though he was most definitely a warrior of fearsome strength and skill, Musashi was also a product of the times, living in a brutal era in which killings among martial artists were far more common.

For many modern-day followers of Japanese martial arts, Musashi's embrace of the philosophical side of Budo, his writings, his incredible martial skills, and his representation in literature and popular culture have made him into a perfect figurehead for not just Japanese swordsmanship, but martial arts in general. As a result, he is often considered as the benchmark warrior-scholar to which all other Japanese martial artists and tacticians are compared.

Embodying Philosophical Elements of *Budō*

For practitioners of Budo, be it swordsmanship, archery, Judo, Kendo, or any other art that falls under this umbrella, Musashi's legend embodies a number of ideals that students can aspire to within their own studies.

For example, in this legend (and other stories of his life) Musashi embodies confidence and courage, yet is not without morality. He studies scholarly materials and incorporates what he learns into his approaches. Finally, he also utilizes his own intelligence rather than pure martial skills to overcome his opponent.

All of the above are highlighted with great importance in Musashi's writing and many of the works he influenced. Some may even argue that these philosophical ideals are more relevant to modern life, and therefore the true meaning of martial arts, than pure fighting skills.

Finally, as a swordsman, poet, painter, author, and philosopher of great renown, Musashi's legend sets an extremely high bar. One which anyone who is serious about studying Japanese Budo and the related history, culture, philosophies or martial techniques may aspire to.

A woodblock print of the legendary battle by artist Yoshifusa
Utagawa, painted between 1843 and 1847.

References & Figures

[1] As described in the "Nitenki" version of events. Tokitsu, K. (2006). *Miyamoto Musashi: His Life and Writings*. Weatherhill. p. 77

[2] Tokitsu. (2006).

[3] Wilson, W. S. (2013). *The Lone Samurai: The life of Miyamoto Musashi*. Shambhala. p. 40.

[4] Wilson. (2013). p. 8.

[5] Musashi, M. (2018). *The Book Of Five Rings: A Classic Text on the Japanese Way of the Sword*. (T. F. Cleary, Trans.). Shambhala. p. 4.

[6] Tokitsu. (2006). p. 7.

[7] De Lange, W. (2019). *Miyamoto Musashi: The Battle of Sekigahara*. Retrieved November 24, 2021, from http://www.miyamotomusashi.eu/battles/the-battle-of-sekigahara.html.

[8] Yoshikawa, E. (1993). *Musashi*. Tokyo: Kodansha International, 1993.

[9] Tokitsu. (2006). p. 77.

[10] Tokitsu. (2006). p. 37.

[1] Musashi. (2018). p. 4.

[12] Tokitsu. (2006). p. 87.

[13] Wilson. (2013). p. 40.

[14] Green, T. A. (2001). *Martial Arts of the World: An Encyclopedia*. ABC Clio. p. 762.

Page 100 photo adapted from Roger Ferland's image, Duel between Sasaki Kojiro and Miyamoto Musashi. Sourced from Flickr.

The image on page 107 is public domain.

Part III: Duels

HELIO GRACIE

Grapplers from the East and West Meet

Helio Gracie was born in the city of Belem, Northern Brazil, in 1913. He was the sixth child out of eight—five brothers and three sisters. Helio was weaker and frailer than his older brothers in his youth and as a result was not allowed to participate in Jiu Jitsu training alongside his siblings until he was sixteen. Helio then allegedly trained in Judo and Koryu (traditional) Jiu Jitsu alongside his brothers under an expert grappler named Mitsuyo Maeda.

Standing at five-foot-seven, with a thin but muscular frame, Helio was far from the frail figure that is often described in the stories of his life. Many public images of Helio Gracie are those taken in his later years, which may account for this reputation, as he appears much thinner than he was in his youth.

Helio Gracie died on January twenty-ninth, 2009, in Petrópolis, Brazil. He was ninety-five, and had continued training and teaching until ten days before his death, when he suddenly became ill.

He is now known as the founder of Gracie Jiu Jitsu, Tenth-degree Grandmaster of Jiu Jitsu and Third-degree black belt in Judo. He is also seen as a pioneer of Brazilian Jiu Jitsu (BJJ) and patriarch of the Gracie family who helped develop early Mixed Martial Arts (MMA) competitions, such as the original UFC contests. Some of the inspiration for these MMA competitions is thought to stem from his and his brothers' participation in cross-style, *Vale Tudo* (no-holds barred) matches in Brazil during the early twentieth century.

Helio's lineage of Jiu Jitsu promotes a self-defense-based style, while his brother Carlos's lineage is more focused on sport and competition. The Grandmaster fathered ten children, who helped to cement his legacy, many becoming famous martial artists in their own right, such as Royce, Rorian, and Rickson Gracie.

THE LEGEND

The crowd erupted into a ground-shaking roar as Helio stepped out into the bright lights of the newly built *Maracanã* Stadium on October twenty-third, 1951.

The air was heavy with humidity and sweat; it was a warm autumn evening and the crowd was two hundred thousand strong. People thronged into every seat in the stadium.

Along with thousands of Helio's countrymen were dozens of celebrities, sportsmen, and more reporters than he could count. Rumor had it that both the President and Vice President would also be among the crowd. The sound coming from the spectators made it seem as though half of Brazil had turned up, desperate to see their homegrown hero take on the greatest Judo fighter on the face of the planet.

Masahiko Kimura stood in the center of the ring, awaiting his opponent. The Japanese Judoka looked far bigger than Helio remembered, somewhere close to two hundred twenty pounds by his reckoning, while he was closer to one hundred fifty.

What's more, Kimura was waging a serious vendetta against Helio. After he had choked Yukio Kato, Kimura's friend and teammate, unconscious in that same ring less than a month before, he had become despised in Japan for sullying the reputation of the Japanese martial arts community.

Helio's patriotic supporters had only made things worse by carrying a fake coffin up to Kimura's corner a few minutes before he came out, to signify that the Judo fighter's reputation was about to be well and truly murdered by their own hero.

This was a daunting situation to be in, but having grown up in the slums of Belem, taking on all challengers in both the street and the ring since he was a teen, Helio knew Kimura was just one more obstacle he had to overcome. Just a few days before, the Japanese fighter had announced to the press that he would consider the Brazilian the winner if "he could even last three minutes."[1]

This looked like it might well become the defining match of Helio's career, and as he prepared with his brother Carlos, he told him that merely surviving the fight was not his plan at all. He was going to do the impossible and win!

The Brazilian climbed into the ring, with his brothers and training partners in his corner, cheering him on. The bell rang, signaling the first of a planned three ten-minute rounds. Helio had always preferred to fight with no time limits, playing with his opponents like a chess game, waiting for his moment to take the advantage. While there were going to be three rounds, at least in this bout there would be no points or scoring; only a knockout or submission would seal the win.

The pair immediately came into a clinch, pulling one another forward and backward, each trying to shift their opponent off balance and gain a takedown. Helio moved to sweep Kimura's legs from under him, but his opponent's size and strength, coupled with his experience as a top-tier Judoka, made it near impossible for him to be taken down.

Kimura quickly replied with a barrage of his own techniques, throwing the smaller man around like a rag doll, smashing him against the floor over and over, hoping to end the fight with a knockout. Helio's head was spinning, every inch of his body burning from impact with the ground, but the soft matted floor had saved him from serious injury, at least so far.

Kimura, seeing that his efforts weren't working, pinned Helio to the mat and tried to submit him using chokes and leverage. But this was where the Brazilian thrived. Helio had never had the size, strength, or power of his brothers, but on the mat, his technique ruled supreme. Helio slid and maneuvered out of every attempt his opponent made to finish the fight, the pair still going move-for-move and counter-to-counter when the bell rang.

Helio's arms, legs, and lungs were on fire from exertion as he retired to his corner. His Japanese adversary sat still and stoic across the ring, as if he had just taken a gentle stroll rather than engaged in a ten-minute contest of wills. The Brazilian shook off his apprehension. He was under the gaze of an entire nation and couldn't let them down.

The bell chimed and the pair met again on the canvas. Quick as a cat, Kimura swept Helio and once again took him down, determined to prove himself by picking up right where they had left off.

The Judoka pinned his opponent in a North-South hold, with his head against Helio's chest and vice versa. Kimura's weight was crushing, and suddenly the Brazilian was struggling for breath. There were glimpses of bright lights pulsing overhead as the dark grip of unconsciousness began to swallow his thoughts.

In a last-ditch attempt to break free, Helio forced an arm between them, giving him a tiny fraction of space to breathe. This turned out to be a fatal mistake. Kimura seized the limb and applied a double-joint armlock, wrenching against his shoulder. A burst of searing agony shot through the smaller man as both bone and tendons snapped, but he refused to give in.

Kimura wrenched again. There was a second pop of something giving in his body and suddenly Helio felt nothing other than the room spinning. He gritted his teeth and tried to break free from the Japanese fighter's hands, but his grip was iron.

Kimura holds Gracie in "Kesa-gatame" (a scarf hold), minutes before applying the winning technique.

Helio Gracie

The next thing Helio knew, Carlos was standing over him. Kimura was already up on the ropes with his arms raised. Their battle was over.

The Brazilian had lost the match, but his spirit had never waned. Through sheer strength of will, refusing to give up even in the face of certain defeat and surviving not only three minutes, but more than fifteen, the Jiu Jitsu master had earned the respect of a nation.

THE FACTS

Although much of Helio Gracie's tale is well-recorded, there are several areas of debate surrounding both the Master's early training and his legendary fight with Kimura.

The first of these misconceptions begins with Mitsuyo Maeda, the Gracie brothers' Jiu Jitsu teacher. Various members of the Gracie clan perpetuate the story that Maeda was a student of traditional Koryu Jiu Jitsu (a traditional battlefield form), possibly to create an aura of intrigue and exoticism surrounding their system.[2]

In reality, records confirm there is no evidence for the claim that Maeda studied anything other than Judo, in which he was a fourth Dan (degree) black belt. That said, prior to World War Two, the rankings for Judo only went up to seventh Dan. Therefore, this indicates that Maeda had an exceptional skill level.[3]

It is often cited that Helio was frail and weak as a child. This plays well into the ethos of Gracie Jiu Jitsu being effective for weaker practitioners and gives a reason for the master to prefer engaging with Kimura (and others) on the ground rather than in standing combat. However, it is known that during his youth, Helio Gracie was a skilled swimmer and rower, while some scholars also suggest that he was simply not interested in training, so he feigned weakness and lethargy.[4]

In relation to his legendary 1951 fight with Kimura, it appears that several details in this tale have been exaggerated over time to make the story more compelling. While the Gracies' version of events often claims that Kimura had a huge weight advantage, most independent estimates state that it could only have been twenty to thirty pounds at most.[5] As there were no weigh-ins before the match, however, these discrepancies are difficult to verify.

While Kimura allegedly stated that he would consider Helio the winner if he could last three minutes, this is doubtful for several reasons. First, the claim comes from a Gracie-produced documentary;[6] second, Kimura's tactics of throwing Helio against padded mats were unlikely to be the strategy of someone attempting to win by knockout; and finally, neither of the participants shared a common tongue.

Kimura also confirmed this sentiment himself in his autobiography. He stated that during the first round he intended to give the audience a show, in particular those who were upset by Kato's loss just one month before, rather than finish the match quickly.[7]

Helio also later claimed that he expected to lose going into the match and simply wanted to test his skills against the greatest grappler on the planet.[8] Although it is not possible to know for sure how the Brazilian felt prior to the bout, his followers carrying in a fake coffin for his opponent demonstrates that there was not a clear expectation that he was the underdog of the challenge.

Finally, the claims that the bout attracted two hundred thousand spectators are unsubstantiated. The newly built Maracanã Stadium was one of the biggest in the world, with a capacity of approximately that number; however, the fight is actually estimated to have attracted just twenty thousand spectators.[9] Therefore, it was not the type of nation-vs-nation, fighting-for-honor bouts we see in movies but a much smaller and less significant affair altogether. However, twenty thousand was still a phenomenal number of spectators for a newly emerging sport that had just a fraction of the recognition and reputation it does today.

While the spectacle of one of the greatest grappling matches in history is obviously entertaining, it ended with a decisive loss for the Gracie clan.

The statements that followed from Helio about wanting to test himself or outlast three minutes by refusing to give in cleverly turned the Brazilian Master's worst loss into a heroic moral victory. This ethos has played a role in developing the Gracie Jiu Jitsu patriarch's reputation, and helped to elevate him to legendary status within the minds of his followers.

In contrast to this image of a wise man ahead of his time, it should be noted that Helio had a firm sense of machismo and homophobia, and also expressed extremely controversial views in several interviews. For example, he openly compared those who were HIV positive to "dogs" and stated they were deserving of their affliction, and that sex should only ever be used for procreation.[10]

While Helio Gracie's attitudes may be due in part to the times in which he was raised and his religious background, the Brazilian Master was in other areas very forward-thinking and progressive. In the author's opinion, however, personal attributes should always be considered when identifying a role-model for martial artists to aspire to emulate.

Functions of the Legend

Providing Rationale for Technical Aspects of BJJ

Despite the outcome of the event, Helios' legendary battle against Kimura still serves a number of purposes today. Most obviously, it emphasizes certain physical aspects of the martial arts, such as the technique Helio's opponent used to defeat him in the match (now known simply as "the Kimura" among BJJ practitioners).

However, Helio's legend also provides reasons for the development of modern BJJ and the ground-oriented approach to fighting, rather than emphasizing sweeps and throws like Kimura's Judo, as well as focusing on leverage and angles rather than sheer size or strength.

Helio was often outweighed by his brothers and opponents, such as Kimura, and had to rely on physics and technique to overcome these disadvantages. Similarly, he was of a lean physique and likely would not tire as quickly as stronger and heavier opponents (although this appeared to be untrue in Kimura's case). This logic, however, provides a rationale for Helio's preference to face opponents on the floor for extended periods of time rather than standing.

Embodying the Philosophies of BJJ

The legendary battle between Gracie and Kimura underpins a great deal of the ethos of modern-day Brazilian Jiu Jitsu; for example, the bravery and commitment of going up against an opponent despite weight, size, or even gender differences (highlighting again that pure physical strength is often second to the core principles of BJJ).

This tale also embodies the attitudes of BJJ and, by extension, mixed martial arts. These include perseverance and strength of will, displayed by Helio's agreeing to the match knowing there was very little chance he would prevail and his refusal to give up during the bout.

Such elements are often highlighted in modern training schools. In my own experiences with the sport, however, this is not always a good thing. While some practitioners may find pride in emulating Helio and others' feats by refusing to "tap," there are often negative implications where real injury occurs in training because of techniques being applied fully rather than in reduced conditions. This is exemplified by the alarming number of strokes that occur among BJJ practitioners who are choked out too frequently rather than admitting defeat. Compression on the neck, such as that found in the "rear-naked choke" is in fact one of the leading causes of strokes in those aged under forty-five.[11] Therefore, in this light, it seems Helio's legend may actually serve better as a cautionary tale, warning BJJ practitioners only to offer resistance up to a point.

Establishing Lineage for BJJ

Regardless of the bout's outcome, Helio's comments in the local press, or responses to Kimura in the following months or years, Helio Gracie's legend certainly establishes him as an extremely tough and versatile fighter, whom modern-day practitioners can aspire to emulate, in terms of technical skills at the very least.

Furthermore, the legacy that has extended from Helio's ten children, many of whom are highly accomplished fighters he trained directly, has helped cement BJJ's lineage into the realms of modern-day legend.

A variation of "The Kimura" that uses leverage to put pressure on both the shoulder and elbow joints.

References & Figures

[1] Pedreira, R. (2014). *Choque: The Untold Story of Jiu-Jitsu in Brazil, Volume 1 1856-1949*. GTR Publications.

[2] Snowden, J., & Shields, K. (2010). *The MMA Encyclopedia*. ECW. p. 40.

[3] Snowden & Shields (2010).

[4] Pedreira, R. (2016, March 16). *Myths and Misconceptions about Brazilian Jiu-Jitsu*. Global Training Report 2021. Retrieved November 25, 2021, from http://global-training-report.com/myths.htm.

[5] Snowden & Shields (2010). p. 64

[6] Stated in the documentary *Helio Gracie Biography* (2011) by Pedro Valente Jr.–an instructor of Helio's lineage. (27.12). Retrieved November 25, 2021, from https://youtu.be/jo6sG1UqQAs.

[7] Pedreira. (2016).

[8] Stated by Rener Gracie (02.05s) in Gracie Jiu-Jitsu Academy. (2012). *Gracie vs. Kimura—October 23, 1951 (Maracanã Stadium—Rio de Janeiro, Brasil)*. *YouTube*. Retrieved November 25, 2021, from https://www.youtube.com/watch?v=gErppdxesiw.

[9] Snowden & Shields (2010). p. 40.

[10] Magarian, D., & Pedeira, R. (2015, May 26). *Interview with Helio Gracie From Playboy (Brazilian Edition) February 2001*. Roberto Pedreira Global Training Report 2021. Retrieved November 25, 2021, from http://www.global-training-report.com/Helio2.htm.

[11] Demartini, Z., Jr, Rodrigues Freire, M., Lages, R. O., Francisco, A. N., Nanni, F., Maranha Gatto, L. A., &

Koppe, G. L. (2017). Internal Carotid Artery Dissection in Brazilian Jiu-Jitsu. *Journal of Cerebrovascular and Endovascular Neurosurgery, 19*(2), 111–116. https://doi.org/10.7461/ jcen.2017.19.2.111

The image on page 113 is public domain.

The image on page 119 is from the author's personal collection.

BRUCE LEE

Fighting for the Freedom to Teach Kung Fu

Bruce Lee was born on November twenty-seventh, 1940, in San Francisco, while his parents were on tour as opera performers. Lee's family returned to Hong Kong where the youth lived, studied martial arts, and was cast in numerous films.

As a teen, Bruce Lee trained in Wing Chun under Grandmaster Yip Man. At this time, he was well-known as a neighborhood troublemaker who had frequent run-ins with rival Kung Fu schools and the law. With his college prospects looking bleak in Hong Kong, his family sent him to the USA to continue his studies in 1959.

In the USA he trained intermittently in boxing, Judo, Arnis, and various other styles, which all contributed to his development of Jeet Kune Do (The Way of the Intercepting Fist).

Although of above-average height, Bruce's most notable feature was his frame, which was incredibly muscular with an extremely low percentage of body fat. In particular, the extreme size of some body parts, such as his Latissimus Dorsi muscles ("lats"), have led to speculation from modern bodybuilders that he may have supplemented his gym regimen with steroid use.

Bruce Lee died on July twentieth, 1973, aged thirty-two, in Hong Kong. The official cause of death is stated as cerebral edema (swelling and bleeding of the brain) thought to have been triggered by a reaction to the painkiller Equagesic.

He is known as the founder of Jeet Kune Do, winner of multiple film awards, named by *Time Magazine* as "one of the most influential figures of the twentieth century," author of several books on martial arts, poet, and philosopher.

The Legend

"Is this really what you want?" Bruce asked, looking at the ornate letter of challenge in his hand.

"No, but it is what they want."[1] Wong Jack-Man, dressed in the black robes of a Northern Shaolin monk, nodded toward the senior members of the Chinatown martial arts association that had recruited him to champion their cause.

Like Bruce, Jack-Man was a young and highly skilled fighter from Hong Kong, but unlike his opponent, he was willing to uphold the ideals of the association for the glory of traditional martial arts and Chinese culture.

James Lee, a friend and mentor to Bruce and one of the few other progressive martial arts masters on the scene, closed the door of the dilapidated building and slid the bolt across the lock.

Although they had never met before, the rivalry between the two young and upcoming martial arts experts in San Francisco's Chinatown was ready to reach a climax.

It had all begun with Lee's performances at local martial arts exhibitions, where he would show the tremendous power of his one-inch-punches and two-finger pushups.

When Bruce started to claim publicly that most of what was being taught in Chinatown was "nonsense," this got his critics fired up. Finally, he spoke publicly at an exhibition stating, "I would like to let everybody know that any time my Chinatown brothers want to try out my Wing Chun, they are welcome to come find me at my school in Oakland."[2]

This had been the final straw for the old guard, who were already uneasy about Bruce's openness to teach Chinese martial arts to Westerners, many of whom treated them with disdain or viewed their martial arts practices as laughable.

The two squared off in the center of the makeshift arena. Jack-Man bowed with his hands raised at face height, the left clasped over the right in a formal show of respect. Bruce responded with the slightest of nods.

"No striking the eyes or throat. No kicking in the groin," said Jack-Man.

"No. As far as I'm concerned you came here to challenge me, so it's no-holds barred," Bruce replied.[3]

Knowing he couldn't back down in front of the gathered entourage and observers, the challenger agreed.

Bruce slid into his orthodox Wing Chun stance, a southern style of Kung Fu focused on fast, short-range strikes and close-range combat. He moved one foot forward, bending his back knee but keeping his shoulders square, providing a stance that supported his body like a wedge that could be driven forward with ease but would resist when pushed upon.

From this position Bruce could focus on controlling his opponent's center line, a key principle of style that exposed his enemy's vital targets to attack.

In response, Wong stepped wide and deep, falling into a classical stance of Northern Shaolin, a style that emphases range of motion with high kicks and long strikes, better suited to the lanky frames of those from Northern China.

Bruce exploded forward with a series of lightning-fast vertical punches aimed at Jack-Man's face, knowing that the elements of surprise and aggression were crucial components that could be used to one's advantage when facing a strong enemy.

Despite Jack-Man's reactions, which were sharp as a knife, one of the strikes made it through and clipped his face just under the eye. The Northern Shaolin master immediately countered with a swinging strike of his own that narrowly missed Bruce's face and landed on his clavicle with a heavy thud. An explosion of pain coursed through Bruce's chest and neck.

Enraged by the near miss, Bruce decided he had to finish the fight there and then and retaliated with a furious barrage of straight-line chain punches and low kicks, forcing Jack-Man to retreat and take a defensive position.

Less than a minute passed while Lee forced his opponent into a state of retreat, backing up around the makeshift arena. In his haste to defend and wait for an opening, Jack-Man lost his footing and fell to the ground.

Lee pounced on him, seizing the moment of advantage and delivered a dozen hard Wing Chun punches ito Jack-Man's back and head while he fought to cover up and protect himself.

"Have you had enough?" Bruce shouted down at his opponent, who refused to answer. Lee pounded some more. "Have you had enough?!"[4] Finally, with no way to defend himself and at the mercy of the Wing Chun fighter, Jack-Man had no choice but to admit defeat.

Bruce backed off and the stunned crowd quickly dispersed. Those who had favored Jack-Man muttered and groaned amongst themselves in defeat as they made their way home.

Sometime later, Bruce's wife Linda found her husband sitting outside on the steps at the back of the warehouse. He was gazing off into the distance, despondent about what was a decisive victory.

When Linda asked what was wrong, Bruce explained. He told her how he was disappointed with himself for letting the fight drag on so long, and that it should have been over in seconds. Instead, he'd gotten to the point of being unusually exhausted and injured from the victory.

Bruce glanced down to his knuckles that had swollen to nearly twice their size and wondered why his system was so reliant on hand strikes. Why did it requir him to stay in close range, chest forward, where it was hard to generate power rather than using twisting motions, like boxers and even Karate masters. Why did his style, which seemed so crisp and efficient in training, suddenly feel so ineffective and slow?

Sitting with his wife, tired and contemplative, Lee made the decision there and then that he needed to adapt. Hed had to come up with his own methodology, his own practice, taking the best from all worlds to create not just a new style of martial arts, but a new approach to martial arts itself. This would eventually become the "Way of the Intercepting Fist"—"Jeet Kune Do."

THE FACTS

While the tale of the duel between Lee and Jack-Man has been told countless times in various formats and platforms, this iteration seems to prevail most of all.

Most likely this particular legend rose to popularity due to its wide distribution in Linda Lee's books, which were immensely popular in the years following Bruce's death, and the dramatic interpretation of events which could have sprung from one of his movies. In particular, this is supported by the underpinning argument about race and the teaching of Chinese martial arts to Westerners, which creates a hero of Lee and villain of Jack-Man.

This claim was originally made by Linda Lee, who said "Three other Chinese accompanied Wong Jack-Man, who handed Bruce an ornate scroll which appeared to have been an ultimatum from the San Francisco martial arts community. Presumably, if Bruce lost the challenge, he was either to close down his institute or stop teaching Caucasians."[5]

This story was then cemented in the public psyche over the coming years through many retellings, many of which heightened the drama to ridiculous proportions. Most notable was the 1993 film *Dragon: A Bruce Lee Story*, where the hero had to face "a real killer"[6] before a panel of old Chinese Kung Fu masters to earn the right to teach whomever he desired. This scene took place in what appears to be a secret underground Kung Fu battle arena that was allegedly somewhere in downtown San Francisco (rather than Bruce Lee's own school at 4157 Broadway, which is now a Toyota dealership).[7]

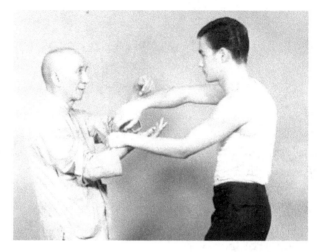

Bruce Lee performs Chi Sao (sticking hands) techniques with
Grandmaster Yip Man, in Hong Kong.

Throughout the fight, Bruce performs nothing even slightly
reminiscent of Wing Chun and instead appears to act as a
culmination of his persona in later films. It should be noted,
though, that they at least went to the effort of changing the
name of the character based on Jack-Man (probably in the
hope of avoiding a defamation lawsuit).

It is most likely true that Lee did not buy into the racial
exclusion that was no doubt an issue of the times (he was
married to a Caucasian woman and was mixed race himself,
as it is generally accepted that his maternal grandmother was
European[8]). However, it is a stretch to infer from this that all
other schools of Chinese martial arts in the San Francisco area
were exclusively of Chinese ethnicity.

Although this Chinese-exclusive culture of martial arts
teaching likely *did* happen in years prior, a number of Western
students studied in Chinatown by the 1960s, even including
some well-known martial artists such as Ed Parker.

As one scholar notes, there is substantial evidence that the old code of keeping Chinese martial arts secretive was "well into its final throes by the time of the Bruce Lee–Wong Jack-Man showdown."[9]

Meanwhile, Jack-Man himself has vehemently denied this as a reason for their conflict for over fifty years and continued to do so up until his death in 2017, stating, "What (Linda) wrote is absolutely not true. What provoked the fight was Bruce Lee's arrogance and his insulting treatment of other martial artists. He trashed the teachers in Chinatown, calling them 'old tigers with no teeth' and lectured them about his Wing Chun system being far superior to their traditional Chinese martial arts."[10]

While the duel was likely not a battle over whom to teach and whom not to teach, it is reasonable to consider that Jack-Man was seen as representing the traditional masters and styles of Chinatown, while Bruce was the voice of change.[11]

Regarding the physical aspects of the fight, in a 1967 interview in *Black Belt Magazine* Bruce stated:

"I'd gotten into a fight in San Francisco (a reference, no doubt, to the Bay Area rather than the city) with a Kung Fu cat, and after a brief encounter the son-of-a-bitch started to run. I chased him and, like a fool, kept punching him behind his head and back. Soon my fists began to swell from hitting his hard head. Right then I realized Wing Chun was not too practical and began to alter my way of fighting."[12]

While he does not name Wong specifically in this interview, it seems from both its timing, similarities to Linda Lee's descriptions, and the other documented bouts he had that Bruce was referring to the same event.

However, it is worth speculating whether this version of events would be a significant enough catalyst to make Bruce completely drop a style of martial arts he had been learning for more than a decade already, especially if he had defeated a renowned martial artist, who many considered to be the more likely victor[13] with a decisive victory.

While there are a limited number of confirmed firsthand accounts of the fight, they tend to fall into one of two camps, the first of which tells a story reminiscent of Bruce and Linda's, and the second of which is far less one-sided.

Jack-Man claims the fight "lasted at least twenty minutes, maybe twenty-five."[14] This length might also explain why Bruce was noted in all accounts (including his own) to be considerably winded.

William Chen, a Tai Chi instructor who witnessed the event, supports this by saying the fight lasted approximately twenty minutes and certainly did not finish with Jack-Man "brought to the floor and pounded into a state of demoralization." He also states that he "remembers the fighters joining on several occasions, but he could not see very clearly what was happening at those moments."[15]

Jack-Man's own descriptions offer a different perspective on the match than that of Lee and his wife, stating that Lee was extremely angry from the outset. David Chin (the mutual friend that helped organize the meeting explains that "it was not a friendly atmosphere" and that "the challenge was real."[16]

This version is further emphasized by Jack-Man's claims that Lee was intent on causing him serious bodily harm, particularly when starting the fight by pretending to shake his hand, then jabbing fingertip strikes at his eyes.

Jack-Man says, "He continued to swear, yell, and utter terrifying sounds as he repeatedly tried to attack my eyes, throat, and groin in between throwing straight punches at my chest."[17]

The physical aspects of a scene more in keeping with these descriptions were later also depicted in the 2016 film *Birth of the Dragon*. Although the film took some artistic liberties in the dramatization of the movie's pivotal scene, it portrayed the duel in a far less one-sided manner. In reference to the duel's depiction, Jack-Man himself said he enjoyed the part when he headlocked Bruce, "which actually happened three times during our fight in 1964."[18]

Also, in the weeks following the bout, rumors started to crop up about the outcome, even though the pair had agreed not to publicly disclose information about the fight.

Jack-Man soon issued a public statement in a local newspaper in response, challenging Bruce's version of events and calling for a public rematch, to which the usually outspoken Bruce Lee did not respond.

Finally, it should be considered that perspectives massively impact our objective opinions, and therefore the realistic outcomes of the fight can be considered part of the mystery. However, they likely fall somewhere between the two camps' tales.

Meanwhile, the spectacle of the actual fight has obviously been far eclipsed by the legend, and regardless of the outcome, one way or another it helped to create a path for what would later become Jeet Kune Do and Bruce's iconic philosophies.

FUNCTIONS OF THE LEGEND

Creating a Cultural Icon

It should be noted that this duel has become one of the most frequently referenced periods of Bruce Lee's life. It has been shown dozens of times in film, retold in hundreds of books and magazines, and been recycled countless times orally. This has elevated it to a piece of pop-culture iconography that has influenced countless works of cinema, television, and storytelling throughout the latter twentieth century.

Although the legend told by various parties differs massively (and both versions of events have featured in various renditions), one theme is consistent throughout. Whether the fight was one-sided or not, it seems clear that Bruce's view of traditional martial arts being antiquated or unrealistic was founded by such fights like this one and the surrounding discussions.

Popularizing Discussion on Martial Arts in the West

The ongoing debate surrounding the effectiveness of different styles and systems of martial arts has long been a topic of discussion in the East. For example, debates surrounding the dominance of Northern and Southern Chinese styles of Kung Fu have been going on for at least five-hundred years.[19]

However, until the rise of figures like Lee, who thought to question the efficacy of traditional systems (inspired by events like his fight with Jack-Man), this was a relatively unquestioned concept in the West, where Eastern styles of martial arts were still relatively new and considered in high regard by the general public.

In this case, the Bruce Lee/Wong Jack-Man duel certainly helped to bring the discussion forward into the twenty-first century, possibly even popularizing the style-versus-style debate among Western audiences for one of the first times.

Teaching Jeet Kune Do Philosophies

Finally, the legend of Bruce Lee's bout with Jack-Man can be seen as a modern-day parable for others, serving as the catalytic moment for the development of Lee's philosophy that states: "Absorb what is useful, discard what is not, add what is uniquely your own."[20]

This is particularly relevant for modern-day martial artists, who have access to a wide range of sources and can identify what is likely to work in their own training and what is not.

This philosophy further underpins what later became the ethos of modern mixed martial arts. Some consider Lee as the "godfather" of MMA for this reason. Personally, I feel that this is a natural evolution of martial arts, and things are now evolving further with striking and wrestling making a comeback against the once-dominant system of BJJ. However, without the tinder of Lee's huge name, appealing legend, and duel to have sparked it off, we may certainly be years behind where martial arts are today.

"The Chasse Bas" was incorporated into Jeet Kune Do from "Savate" (French Kickboxing). It serves as a jabbing or checking low sidekick and is seen frequently throughout Lee's films.

References & Figures

[1] Lee, L. (1975). *The Life and Tragic Death of Bruce Lee*. Star Books. p. 37.

[2] Russo, C., & Lee, S. (2019). *Striking Distance: Bruce Lee & the Dawn of Martial Arts in America*. University of Nebraska Press. p. 133.

[3] Ibid.

[4] Lee, L. (1975). *The Life and Tragic Death of Bruce Lee*. Star Books. p. 37.

[5] Dorgan, M. (1980, July). "Bruce Lee's Toughest Fight." *Official Karate*. p. 1.

[6] *Dragon: The Bruce Lee Story*. (1995.). Retrieved May 20, 2022, from https://www.youtube.com/watch?v=AU9fdSjbeRo. (0.20s).

[7] Bruce Lee. LocalWiki. (2013, March 11). Retrieved April 21, 2022, from https://localwiki.org/oakland/Bruce_Lee.

[8] Chin, J. W. (2017). "Striking Distance: Bruce Lee & the Dawn of Martial Arts in America." *Sport in Society* 21(3): 574–576. doi:10.1080/17430437.2017.1379187. p. 576.

[9] Russo & Lee. (2019). *Striking Distance*. p. 147.

[10] Dorgan, M. (2017). *Shaolin Master Wong Jack Man's Last Interview*. Hunyuan Martial Arts Academy of San Jose. Retrieved April 18, 2022, from https://www.taichisanjose.com/wong-jack-man-interview. p. 1.

[11] Russo & Lee. (2019). *Striking Distance*. p. 139.

[12] Vaughn, J., & Lee, M. (1986). *The Legendary Bruce Lee*. Ohara Publications. p. 6.

[13] Russo & Lee. (2019). *Striking Distance*. p. 136

[14] Dorgan. (1980). *Bruce Lee's Toughest Fight*. Para 15.

[15] Dorgan. (1980). *Bruce Lee's Toughest Fight*. Para 15.

[16] Russo, C., & Lee, S. (2019). *Striking Distance: Bruce Lee & the Dawn of Martial Arts in America*. University of Nebraska Press. p. 138.

[17] Dorgan. (2017). *Shaolin Master*. p. 1.

[18] Ibid.

[19] Henning, S. (2018). "Southern Fists and Northern Legs: Geography of Chinese Boxing." In M. Demarco, Ed., *Henning's Scholarly Works on Chinese Combative Traditions* (pp. 34–43). essay, Via Media Publishing.

[20] Little, J., & Lee, B. (2016). *The Warrior Within: The Philosophies of Bruce Lee*. Chartwell Books. p. 181.

The image on page 128 is public domain.

The image on page 134 is from the author's personal collection.

Part IV

CHALLENGES

In this section we will examine some of the challenges that legendary martial artists have taken on. While they may include both mental and physical challenges, there are often overarching themes of human-versus-nature.

The concept of taking on wild animals in particular is seen frequently throughout martial arts histories. Since times of antiquity, facing a powerful animal has often been identified as the ultimate test of legitimacy for a warrior. By succeeding, they therefore demonstrate not just their own skills and wits, but the functionality of their system too.

In the following stories, this theme of human-versus-nature manifests itself in a number of ways, such as taking on the wilderness, wild animals, or even the hero's own fears or self-doubts.

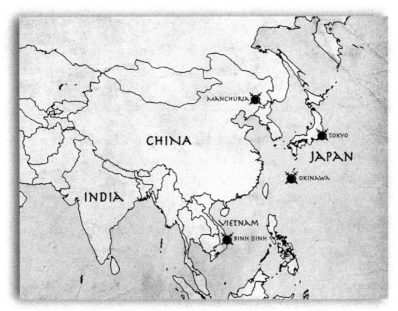

Key sites from Chapter Four: Tokyo and Okinawa (Japan), Manchuria (China) and Binh Dinh (Vietnam)

BÙI THỊ XUÂN
The Swordswoman and the Tiger

Born in 1752 in *Bình Định* Province, Central *Việt Nam*, Bui Thi Xuan was the eldest daughter of a well-off and respected family. However, she caused a stir by bucking societal norms and becoming a martial artist and revolutionary.

She likely trained in Vietnamese and Chinese unarmed systems, and battlefield arts, in particular broadsword and spear. Xuan was also a renowned trainer and leader of elephant cavalry.

Although there are no known paintings of Bui Thi Xuan from her lifetime, historical accounts describe her as being tall and beautiful. A large stature would have been beneficial for her later exploits, such as battling with dual swords and fighting from the back of an elephant—for which she was renowned.

In most modern statues and drawings, we see Xuan either in full battle armor or in a traditional Vietnamese long dress.

She is now known as one of five legendary generals of the *Tây Sơn* Dynasty (a peasant rebellion that took control of Vietnam in the eighteenth century). She is also a matriarch figure of *Võ Cổ Truyền* (Traditional Vietnamese Martial Arts) and the creator of the Phoenix Double Sword style.

Along with her husband, *Trần Quang Diệu,* and their daughter, Xuan was executed for her crimes against the ruling *Nguyễn* Dynasty in the Imperial Citadel, *Huế,* in 1802. Legend has it that Xuan and her daughter were sentenced to be crushed to death beneath the feet of an elephant, while her husband was skinned.

Bui Thi Xuan remains a popular folk hero in Vietnam to this day. Many modern Vietnamese pray to her at ancestral altars and in Taoist temples, alongside other famous female Vietnamese fighters. There are also streets named in Xuan's honor in almost every large city in Vietnam, with statues and temples dedicated to her in her home province of Binh Dinh.

The legendary warrior is also celebrated for refusing to conform to the societal trends of the times, in a manner similar to the semi-mythical Chinese figure Hua Mulan. Instead of becoming a housewife or taking up a typical female role, Xuan rose to be one of the most fearsome warrior generals of her era.

THE LEGEND

It was late afternoon, and the scorching sun was beating down as Tran Quang Dieu reached the forest that lay at the foot of a mountain. He wiped the sweat from his head as he picked his way through the overgrown hunting tracks heading north. The leader of the rebellion, *Nguyên Lưu,* had instructed him personally to stay off the main roads. The letter he carried could not fall into their enemies' hands or all would be lost.

A grassroots rebellion was growing fast in Binh Dinh Province. Dieu, alongside many other peasant soldiers and renowned martial arts experts of the region, had already taken several strategic towns and were building up momentum fast.

Soon they would overthrow the feudal houses who ruled the north and south of the country. The rival Nguyen and *Trịnh* houses had been in a years-long struggle to claim the country, and in doing so had condemned many like him to extreme poverty.

The paths soon grew so thick and overgrown that the sun was all but blocked out by the canopy overhead. When Dieu came to a clearing and spotted a stream running close by, he stopped to take a drink and water his horse. Sitting on the ground with his back against the tree, Dieu suddenly noticed the buzzing of the insects had halted and the calls of nearby birds had stopped. In fact, the jungle was now all but silent. He turned to mount his horse, but without warning, the animal bolted.

The next sound Dieu heard sent a stab of mortal panic through his heart. An unmistakable predator's snarl came from just beyond the thick rushes that lined the river. The soldier leapt to his feet, grabbing for the sword in its sheath on his belt as the tiger came bursting up from the banks.

Before he had a chance to draw his weapon, the beast lunged. Dieu avoided its jaws, but the tiger's claws tore a deep gash into his arm. He screamed in pain and fury as the sheathed sword flew from his hand into the undergrowth. At that moment, Dieu knew he must fight back and force the creature to reconsider. All his years of martial arts training would count for nothing if he did not.

The injured man clambered to his feet, doing his best to keep moving as the tiger advanced. Dieu threw punches and stabs with his fingers at the beast's eyes, trying to keep it at a distance. The tiger was apprehensive, tracking forward and backward, waiting for the perfect moment to strike. Dieu knew he had to stand his ground. The second he turned his back and ran, he would become a mouse to this ferocious cat. But how long could he hold it off? Surely his demise was inevitable.

After almost an hour of this life-and-death game, Dieu was fading fast. The adrenaline had left him exhausted as he swung weakly at the tiger, his arms growing slower and heavier with each strike. In a last-ditch attempt to salvage his life, Dieu charged the creature, hoping he could drive it back.

Instead, the tiger pounced, catching him mid-charge. With its bulk on his torso, pinning Dieu to the floor, the beast sunk its razor-like teeth deep into his shoulder. There was nothing to do now but welcome death, hoping it would come fast to end his agony.

From somewhere in the distance, the rhythmic beat of hooves seemed to echo through the ground, growing in volume with each second. Moments later, a shadowy figure swung down from the horse, landing deftly at his side with a blade in each hand.

Am I dead? Dieu wondered, watching the scene unfold through bloodied eyes. The young woman moved as if some fearsome warrior spirit possessed her, lunging and stabbing with a pair of swords at the tiger.

The creature backed off for a moment before turning its attention back to Dieu; it had worked hard for its kill and was loath to give it up easily.

The young woman shouted, waving her arms and turning her back, provoking the beast into an attack. As the tiger charged, she swung around and slashed with lightning speed, circling and spinning two blades to form an impenetrable barrier of steel.

As the woman pushed forward, the blades cut deep into the beast's face and body. The tiger roared with anger and rolled on the floor with pain before deciding this fight was not worth its life. With a final snarl toward the couple, the creature fled into the jungle.

* * *

When Quang Dieu awakened in a nearby village a day later, he didn't know what to make of the situation. Who was the mysterious figure to whom he owed his life? Soon after, a young woman came walking through the door of the hut and his question was answered.

Quang Dieu was at a loss for words. Xuan was so soft, calm, and stunningly beautiful. He found it hard to believe she was the warrior that had fought with such magnificent fury and skill for his life.

It did not take long for the pair of fighters to fall in love and marry. Together, they rose high in the ranks of the Tay Son rebel militia.

Xuan became famous for her military prowess, developing all-female squadrons of soldiers and teaching them her double sword fighting style. She also trained squads of elephant-mounted warriors, while Dieu played a crucial role as a general of the rebellion. The Tay Son rebels eventually took control of the country, forming the first incarnation of what is modern-day Vietnam.

THE FACTS

While there are many written and oral records of Bui Thi Xuan's exploits, most of which have aspects of truth to them, she was a relatively unknown figure until her story was "revived" on the printed page in 1928 in two separate books about Vietnamese heroines.[1]

When discussing Xuan's martial arts training, it is widely accepted that her particular location was a hotbed of martial arts activity during the early-nineteenth century. Binh Dinh Province was home to some of the great warrior clans of Vietnamese history; most notably the *Trương* who had ventured south as the flag bearers of the Nguyen Dynasty. The Truong clan is typically credited with developing the forms of traditional Vietnamese Kung Fu (known as Vo Co Truyen).[2]

According to local records, Xuan trained with martial arts experts in the villages of *An Vinh* and *Thuận Truyền*, both of which had their own specific combat traditions. The first is famed for unarmed fighting, the second for staff fighting.[3]

There were also several renowned Chinese martial artists in the province at the time, meaning that the methods studied by Xuan and her fellow members of the Tay Son Rebellion were likely to have blended traditional Vietnamese warfare practices with those from their northern neighbors.[4] This conclusion is supported by the types of weapons found in Vo Co Truyen, many of which mirror those used in the Chinese battlefield arts of the day.

There are no clear, provable sources that can either confirm or deny that Xuan met Tran Quang Dieu by saving him from a tiger, other than oral histories. However, written versions were later popularized in various poems and stories from the region.

Most notable was the work of *Nguyễn Bá Huân* (1848–1899) who famously detailed the battle with the tiger in his work "Tales of a Headscarf Heroine," which was itself based upon oral retellings.[5] Although this specific part of Xuan's legend is not provable, many cases of tiger attacks were well documented in the wild and untamed lands of central Vietnam during the era. Even today, such incidents remain in living memory, and some groups still carry blades to deter the predators,[6] so it is not implausible.

While it is possible that this was a real event, there is the question of why this incident is so heavily emphasized when compared to both Xuan and Dieu's roles as successful generals in the Tay Son Rebellion.[7] Particularly as this was an event which helped shape the entirety of mainland Southeast Asia—with the rebels dominating both Vietnam and seizing a large part of the Khmer Kingdom (modern-day Cambodia)—just a few short years later.

Xuan's legend is also of interest as it subverts audience expectations by switching the positions of the typical "damsel in distress" narrative. Instead, it casts a well-off, attractive female as the protagonist, rescuing a helpless male victim. In this respect, Bui Thi Xuan's legend sits within an arsenal of Vietnamese female warrior tales that have been used to inspire patriotism and opposition to foreign rule since the early half of the nineteenth century.

Other such tales include the ancient warrior sisters *Hai Bà Trưng* and the anti-French fighter *Võ Thị Sau*—all of whom also died as martyrs.

The French essentially ruled Vietnam by controlling Nguyen Dynasty puppet-monarchs between 1885 and 1953.[8] Some believe that the growing anti-colonialist movements of the late 1920s and 1930s specifically brought Xuan's legend back into vogue as a planned and controlled dissemination of resistance narratives. Marr calls this "a conscious slap to the puppet court in Hue, since Xuan had led Tay Son armies against the Nguyen more than a century before".[9]

Shrines of Bui Thi Xuan and Tran Quang Dieu, where they are worshipped side-by-side, at a temple in Binh Dinh Province, Central Vietnam.

FUNCTIONS OF THE LEGEND

Legitimizing Vietnamese Martial Arts

While the Vietnamese systems of martial arts are less well-known internationally than their Chinese or Southeast Asian counterparts, they have significant followings in Vietnam, the USA, and Europe. They are distinguished by their acrobatic movements, speed, and ferocity, blending aspects of Chinese and Southeast Asian fighting styles.[10]

The legend of Xuan defending her future husband from a tiger attack, as well as other tales surrounding the fighter and her Tay Son counterparts, are still considered by scholars to be "immensely consequential for how practitioners would imagine their participation in Vietnamese martial arts."[11]

First, by having Dieu fight a tiger unarmed (in Ba Huan's iteration at least) it serves to legitimize his, and by extension, the Tay Son Rebels' martial arts skills. In the modern day, the fighting styles developed during the Tay Son Rebellion are still seen as the foundation for a large amount of Vietnam's traditional martial arts practices.[12]

Establishing Lineage for Vietnamese Martial Arts

While the unarmed fighting skills of Dieu demonstrate the legitimacy of Vietnamese martial arts, Xuan's role as a fighter (and later military general), helped to establish a lineage for Vietnamese traditional martial arts.

The legend of Xuan and Dieu, alongside others from the region and era, provide local figureheads to which certain techniques and methods can be directly linked, thus differentiating them from Chinese or other equivalent systems practiced in Vietnam during the period.

For example, Xuan's sword fighting skills specifically embody this function by providing a background for a popular traditional martial arts sword fighting style named "Phoenix Double Swords," which is attributed to her. This has also happened with a number of spear, staff and unarmed styles of the era.[13]

Due to many stylistic elements in the contemporary practices however, it is unclear how far the Phoenix Double Swords style that Xuan allegedly developed resembles the historical practice. Therefore, it is possible that the techniques were developed or adapted later and retroactively accredited to Xuan (and other members of the rebellion) to create this lineage when their legends became widespread.

Part IV: Challenges

Promoting and Inspiring Female Fighters

From the author's own experiences living and training in Vietnam for more than a decade, traditional martial arts remain popular practices among young women (especially in comparison to modern combat sports).

These systems of traditional Vietnamese martial arts are typically viewed as both a source of national pride and a show of female independence. Vietnam has a long and varied history with female warrior figures. This legend, and others with similar themes, have functioned as part of an arsenal of female-led narratives that have contributed to developing a fighting ethos for generations of young Vietnamese women.

This function can be seen as a success due to the ongoing veneration of Xuan as martial matriarch. Furthermore, her ideals of bucking societal norms and normalizing the female warrior persona are evident in the huge numbers of Vietnamese women who have taken up arms, subsequently playing crucial roles in twentieth century conflicts.

In modern times, this female warrior tradition continues to be displayed—albeit in times of peace—by a significant proportion of women taking on jobs, roles, or even hobbies (such as martial arts) that are not typically thought of as feminine pursuits.

A female martial artist demonstrates the "Phoenix Double Sword" fighting style, allegedly developed by Bui Thi Xuan.

References & Figures

[1] Marr, D. G. (1984). *Vietnamese Tradition on Trial, 1920–1945.* University of California Press. p. 211.

[2] Phong Phạm. (2013). *Lịch-Sử-Võ-Học-Việt-Nam Từ-Khởi-Nguyên-Đến-Đầ-Thế-Kỷ-Xxi.* NXB-Văn-Hóa-Thông-Tin. p. 172.

[3] Phong (2013).

[4] Roe, A. J. (2020). *The Martial Arts of Vietnam: An Overview of History and Styles.* YMAA Publication Center. p. 83.

[5] *Trần*, H. K. (2020, November 15). "Views from the South–Martial Arts of Vietnam, Part I & Part II." Retrieved November 25, 2021, from "Views from the South—Martial Arts of Vietnam, Part I—Kung Fu Tea" (chinesemartialstudies.com).

[6] When conducting research for my book *The Martial Arts of Vietnam*, I stayed with a family of the *Tày* ethnic minority in the far north of the country, whose farm used to be attacked by tigers; claw marks on the stone hut were still evident.

[7] Dutton, G. E. (2008). *The Tây Sơn Uprising: Society and Rebellion in Eighteenth Century Vietnam.* Silkworm Books. p. 230.

[8] Goscha, C. (2017). *The Penguin History Of Modern Vietnam.* Penguin Books. p. 497

[9] Marr. (1984). p. 211.

[10] Roe. *The Martial Arts of Vietnam.* (2020).

[11] *Trần.* (2020). p. 12.

[12] Roe. *The Martial Arts of Vietnam.* (2020). p. 88–89.

[13] Roe. *The Martial Arts of Vietnam.* (2020). p. 88–89.

The images on page 147 are Creative Commons Images, courtesy of Bùi Thụy Đào Nguyên

The image on page 150 is from the author's personal collection.

Gogen Yamaguchi
From Prisoner of War to One of Japan's Greatest Karateka

Yamaguchi was born in Miyazaki Prefecture on Kyushu (Japan's southernmost main island) on January twentieth, 1909. He was the third son of ten siblings in a middle-class family.

Yamaguchi trained in various styles of Karate in his youth. At university he met the famed Okinawan master and founder of the *Gōjū-Ryū* system, Chojun Miyagi, and his serious training began.

Yamaguchi was small in height, just five-foot-one, but was known for the sense of power he exuded, which made him appear far more powerful than his stature. Long flowing black hair coupled with the robes he always wore and the way he appeared to glide when he walked led to his nickname "The Cat."

Yamaguchi died on May twentieth, 1989, aged eighty. He is known for bringing Goju-Ryu to mainstream success in Japan, being named as the successor to Chojun Miyagi (according to some sources), creating Karate's free-sparring system, and teaching the first generation of Japanese Karatekas. He is a recipient of the Blue Ribbon Medal of the fifth order of merit for his contributions to the Japanese martial arts.

Although Yamaguchi's legend could be considered in other categories, it has been included in this section as the primary themes of the legend are the physical and mental challenges of returning from war and trying to bring a small Okinawan school to mainstream acceptance in Japan. This is especially notable as Okinawa was a culturally distinct state and only officially became a part of Japan in 1879. The martial arts from the region were often thought of as inferior to the Japanese systems.

THE LEGEND

On his knees, Gogen Yamaguchi bowed, pressing his forehead to the ground in veneration at the shrine of Admiral Togo in Kagoshima, on the tip of the southernmost island of Japan.

The Karate master prayed for the strength of spirit to complete his task. It would be his greatest challenge yet, and after what he had experienced through times of war, that was no mean feat.

* * *

As a captured special operations officer near the end of World War Two, he had spent two years in a Soviet Gulag. There he had eaten nothing but brown bread and water and been beaten daily. When his captors figured out that it was his Karate practice that had been keeping his will alive, he was forced to spend months in solitary confinement in a cell too low to even stand let alone practice his martial arts.

In isolation, the warrior had simply meditated, spending hours upon hours in a trance-like state. After all this had failed to break his spirit, his captors had forced him naked into a cage with an old tiger they had captured in the wild. They expected him to either fall again into one of his trances and get eaten, or fight and die.

This had all gone wrong. Stunning the beast with a furious scream and vicious open-handed strikes at its eyes and throat, Yamaguchi had managed to get behind the tiger and eventually onto its back. From there he'd wrapped an arm around the old but still-lethal creature's neck, gripping it tight, until the beast had finally become passive. After that night, the guards had treated their Japanese prisoner with respect, maybe out of awe or maybe out of fear.

Eventually, Yamaguchi had been released from the camp and returned to his country, only to be haunted by the things he had seen and done. To make things worse, Japan was all but destroyed, his people weak and broken, their honor shattered.

Only then did Yamaguchi vow to take the next step, the only honorable way to proceed—to commit Seppuku. Ritual suicide, as it would have been in old Japan, when a retainer's master was defeated or killed. He would pull the blade of a short sword across his belly and spill his guts onto the ground, the final stand of a warrior who had lost his purpose.

* * *

Yamaguchi stared down at the blade in his hands. Courage had never been something he lacked; he didn't fear the pain or the darkness. It was his destiny.

A moment before he made the cut, Yamaguchi froze. In an instant of transcendent clarity, he realized that death was not his path. There was another way, a better one. Maybe he could restore his peoples' honor. Maybe he could help rebuild a new Japan by disseminating the martial arts of his forebears for the world to see. Now he had a purpose. Yamaguchi did not have to die to be reborn.

From that moment on, Yamaguchi became a deeply spiritual man, training as a Shinto priest, Yogi, and mystic as well as a teacher of Okinawan martial arts.

In this, however, Yamaguchi found he faced another hurdle. The Japanese public felt disdain for Miyagi's style of martial arts, despite their power. The master then realized he must change his approach to allow Goju-Ryu to become mainstream.

Shortly before his death, Grandmaster Chojun Miyagi visited his student in mainland Japan. He called Yamaguchi to his side and softly muttered to him, "Yamaguchi, you will be the successor of Goju-Ryu Karate. I have nothing more to teach you. You must develop Karate in Japan."[1]

Following the parting words of the great Chojun Miyagi, Yamaguchi fought tooth and nail to instill the Okinawan discipline of Karate in mainland Japan. With his creativity and drive at the helm, this soon grew into a powerful movement. Rather than just teaching kata, he developed equipment and rules that would allow practitioners to spar and exchange live techniques. Much like they already did in the Japanese arts of Kendo and Judo. This led to their acceptance on a wider scale.

THE FACTS

First, it should be noted that it is unknown how close Gogen Yamaguchi came to Seppuku. However, different accounts vary ranging from just considering the idea, to actually having the blade in his hands and being on the cusp of taking his own life.[2,3] Either way, if Yamaguchi, who was known for being extremely straight and solemn, claims he gave serious consideration to the idea, then it is likely to be the case.

While Yamaguchi's incarceration for being a spy is often discussed, his exact role in Manchuria is unclear, although it is known that Yamaguchi was sent there as a supporter (and personal friend) of General Kanji Ishihara.

Ishihara himself was a controversial figure who was known to harbor extreme views about the war and the enemies of Japan. He allegedly envisioned creating a harmonious state of Japanese, Chinese, and Mongol citizens in Manchuria, but somewhat inevitably ended with an extremely repressed and ruthlessly exploited local populace.[4] This possibly offers insight into why the Japanese soldiers that were captured may have been subjected to such harsh treatment after the fall of Manchuria to Soviet forces.

As Noble says in summary of Yamaguchi's role in Manchuria, "(He) is not very specific about what his duties entailed, but he comes over as something like a mixture of administrator, trouble-shooter, spymaster, and undercover agent."[5]

Furthermore, although Yamaguchi never mentions in his biography that he was outright tortured,[6] it is reasonable to assume that life in the Soviet Gulag was no picnic. Yamaguchi was likely subjected to harsh conditions, beatings, starvation, and isolation.

However, the tale of Yamaguchi being thrown into a tiger cage seems to be unfounded and is based upon spurious oral tales.

Most scholars on Yamaguchi's life claim that this tale can be traced to the American Karateka and author Peter Urban, who listed a number of semi-mythical tales in his 1967 work *The Karate Dojo: Traditions and Tales of a Martial Art*.[7, 8] Urban's work in particular features an extremely stylized version of Yamaguchi's legend that reads more like fiction than truth. Urban claims the Karate master stunned the beast with his "Kiai" before kicking it in the face and "applying a reverse armbar choke."[9]

As we can see from the previous (and forthcoming) entries in this book, the theme of challenges against animals in martial arts legends are widespread, perhaps none more so than the tiger, which is a go-to device for proving the legitimacy of one's skills. In fact, there have been many claims from animal experts on the near-impossible nature of such a feat. However, as data suggests that the average circumference of a tiger's neck is approximately twenty-seven inches,[10] while the average arm length for someone of Yamaguchi's stature is approximately twenty-six inches, it would be at least physically possible for him to perform an adaptation of a chokehold using both arms. However, common sense suggests that doing so would have been virtually impossible and would probably have resulted in Yamaguchi being mauled to death.

To muddy the waters yet further, Yamaguchi later stated in his autobiography that he *did* have an unarmed encounter with a tiger, although not necessarily the one told by Urban. Yamaguchi wrote, "In Manchuria one day I went away into the mountains and had a fight with a tiger. With bare hands. It was a terrible experience. I repeated this experience later, before witnesses."[11]

In regard to Yamaguchi being named as Chojun Miyagi's successor, this is also a subject of contention for Goju-Ryu practitioners worldwide for a number of reasons. Firstly, it has been acknowledged that Miyagi only ever stayed in mainland

Japan for periods of less than three months. Therefore, there is some debate over whether it would have been possible for Yamaguchi to even learn the whole system of Goju-Ryu or if he would have had to fill in the gaps later using the knowledge of Miyagi's senior students.[12] As a result, some followers of Goju-Ryu believe that Miyagi only placed Yamaguchi as the head of his lineage in mainland Japan, rather than in Okinawa where he had a number of students with whom he had far closer relationships and who had studied with him for far longer.

It is also popular knowledge that at the time of Miyagi Chojun's death, Gogen Yamaguchi's school of Goju-Ryu "was already to an extent dissociated from Miyagi's Okinawan students" and that "in 1950 Yamaguchi had founded the International Karate-do Goju Association (IKGA) with himself as its head regardless of the fact that Miyagi was still alive."[13] Nonetheless, it is known that Yamaguchi certainly innovated the current system of Goju-Ryu after coming to the conclusion that "the strict Okinawan brand of karate, with its ancient Chinese origins, was too static and limited in style."[14]

While other masters, including his own senior Chojun Miyagi, had experimented with protective gear that would allow free sparring (something that was absent from traditional Okinawan Karate at the time), most of the equipment and approaches were not successful, and the concepts of free fighting remained elusive for Okinawan martial arts. Understanding that this was inhibiting Goju-Ryu's acceptance in mainland Japan, Yamaguchi went back to basics and organized a practical method of Karate training based in realism that would not require protective equipment when free sparring. In doing so, he raised the practice of Goju-Ryu closer to the status of other martial arts in Japan, which ultimately led to its acceptance and widespread practice both in the country and internationally.[15]

Gogen demonstrates free sparring with his son Goshi in 1949.

FUNCTIONS OF THE LEGEND

Elevating Yamaguchi's Status

The stories told about Yamaguchi's time in the Gulag and his tiger encounter are near impossible to either prove or disprove without the discovery of further evidence (such as accounts of the officers stationed at the camp). Therefore, we are only left to speculate on their likelihood. However, regardless of how truthful these events are, there are various reasons why such "credulous disciples accept absurdities as truth and weave them into the story."[16] Yamaguchi's legend is an amazing tale that captures the imagination and seems as though it could have been written for Hollywood itself. But it also serves as a demonstration of what his followers might be able to achieve through their own training. As Green states in regard to similar stories of near-superhuman challenges faced by historical martial arts masters, "Such narratives serve not only to deify individuals (usually founders), but to argue for the superhuman abilities that can be attained by diligent practice of the martial arts."[17]

Legitimizing Goju-Ryu Practices

Yamaguchi's spiritual epiphanies and sheer dedication to his art exemplify the type of spirit that is ideal for practitioners in his (and other similar) lineages. Training in traditional Karate often demands a great deal of patience, self-control, and perseverance, for which the development of this indomitable spirit is key. In addition, through the incorporation of physical aspects in Yamaguchi's legend, we are provided with a full demonstration of the breadth and diversity of Goju-Ryu. This includes striking (particularly with open-handed techniques as with the tiger), breathing (Yamaguchi's scream or "Kiai," at least in Urban's version) and grappling techniques such as that Yamaguchi allegedly used to subdue the beast.

Providing Rationale for Modernization

In regard to the master's alleged selection as Chojun Miyagi's successor, this claim lends Yamaguchi's lineage of Goju-Ryu credibility, which has likely helped with its expansion throughout Japan and the rest of the world. However, in the author's opinion, the final part of Yamaguchi's legend holds the most value to the modern Karatekas.

Without developing the competitive elements of Karate through free sparring, it is likely that the popularity of Goju-Ryu and Okinawan martial arts in general would have failed to find a foothold in Japanese society and reach acceptance similar to Judo and Kendo. In this case, it is unlikely that they would have reached such global popularity, let alone become an international sporting event, going so far as to be featured as a special event in the Japan-hosted Olympic Games. Therefore, through Yamaguchi's innovations, we are provided with a rationale for both the initial development and ongoing practice of sport Karate, which is seen, somewhat controversially by some, as the next evolution of the style.

References & Figures

[1] Yamaguchi, G. (1966). *Karate Goju by the Cat*. International Karate-do Goju-Kai. p. 85.

[2] Okami, P. (1983, January). "The Long and Winding Road: History of Goju-Ryu from Its Origin in China to Its Demise (?) in New York City." *Black Belt Magazine*, p. 70–77.

[3] Cramer, M. I. (2018). *The History of Karate and the Masters Who Made it: Development, Lineages, and Philosophies of Traditional Okinawan and Japanese Karate-Do*. Blue Snake Books. p. 134.

[4] Noble, G. (1997). "The Life Story of Karate Master Gogen Yamaguchi." *Dragon Times*.

[5] Noble. (1997). "The Life Story." p. 28

[6] Noble, G. (1997). "Discussion: Legendary Battles with Wild Cats." *Dragon Times*. Retrieved April 24, 2022, from http://www.dragon-tsunami.org/Dtimes/Pages/articlej.htm.

[7] Green, T. A. (2001). *Martial Arts of the World: An Encyclopedia*. ABC Clio. p. 132.

[8] Cowie, R., & Dyson, M. (2016). *A Short History of Karate* (2nd ed.). Kenkyo-ha Goju Karate Kempo Kai. p. 104.

[9] Urban, P. (1967). *The Karate Dojo: Traditions and Tales of a Martial Art*. Tuttle.

[10] *Tiger and Lion Neck Girth*. Animal vs. Animal Forums. (2013, March 5). Retrieved April 24, 2022, from https://www.tapatalk.com/groups/animalvsanimal/tiger-and-lion-neck-girth-t1572.html.

[11] Noble, G. (1997). "Discussion: Legendary Battles with Wild Cats." *Dragon Times*. Retrieved April 24, 2022, from http://www.dragon-tsunami.org/Dtimes/Pages/articlej.htm. Para 5.

[12] Cramer. (2018). *The History of Karate*. p. 135.

[13] Cowie, R., & Dyson, M. (2016). *A Short History of Karate* (2nd ed.). Kenkyo-ha Goju Karate Kempo Kai. p. 34.

[14] "Gogen 'The Cat' Yamaguchi, Head of Goju Karate." *Black Belt Magazine*. (2016, June 29). Retrieved April 24, 2022, from https://blackbeltmag.com/black-belt-flashback-gogen-the-cat-yamaguchi-head-of-goju-karate.

[15] Cramer. (2018). *The History of Karate*. p. 140.

[16] Cowie, R., & Dyson, M. (2016). *A Short History of Karate* (2nd ed.). Kenkyo-ha Goju Karate Kempo Kai. p. 104.

[17] Green, T. A. (2001). *Martial Arts of the World: An Encyclopedia*. ABC Clio. p. 132.

The image on page 159 is public domain.

MASUTATSU OYAMA
Taking on the Wild

Masutatsu (Mas) Oyama was born in Japanese-occupied Korea on July twenty-seventh, 1923. In a bid for safety, his parents sent him to live with an aunt on her farm in Manchuria at a young age.

Oyama trained in Chinese Kempo during his youth under a Manchurian martial arts expert known as "Li." He later achieved a fourth-degree black belt in Shotokan Karate under Gichin Funakoshi, trained in Judo during college, and studied Goju-Ryu Karate under Gogen Yamaguchi and fellow Korean Karateka So Nei-Chu.

Mas Oyama was a short but stocky figure. For most of his life, he was muscular, with a physique resembling that of a powerlifter. Balding in his later years, Oyama had a firm jaw and was renowned for his deep, focused gaze. Oyama died in Tokyo, Japan from lung cancer on April twenty-sixth, 1994.

He is known as the founder of Kyokushin Karate, author of dozens of books on Japanese martial arts, and one of the most notable figures in modern martial arts due to his extreme challenges. As a prolific author of reference books and other instructional materials, many of the details known about Mas Oyama's personal life and challenges have come from his own accounts. This has led to some level of speculation about the authenticity and possible exaggeration of certain elements of his legend.

THE LEGEND

It didn't concern Mas Oyama in the slightest that pictures of him were pinned up in police stations throughout Tokyo. However, the fear and stress it was causing the young man's friends and students was a different matter altogether.

With a chip on his shoulder about the American occupation of Japan and after losing so many of his friends in the war, Oyama had vowed to give his Karate skills the ultimate real-life trial.

He would go out nightly on the streets of post-WWII Tokyo, fighting foreign soldiers and military police. Sometimes he would win the fight, other times he would lose, but thus far, he had managed to evade both capture and death.

It was So Nei-Chu, a fellow Korean Karate master and mentor to Oyama, that finally shook the young man to his senses. Speaking one on one in the empty Goju-Ryu dojo, Nei-Chu told him, "You'd better withdraw from the world. Seek solace in nature. Retreat to some lone mountain hideout and train your mind and body. After two or three years, you will have gained something immeasurable. As the proverb goes, 'Temper the heated iron before it gets cold.' Train yourself in self-discipline before you grow older if you wish to be a great man."[1]

Struck by his mentor's words and seeing the folly of his ways, Oyama turned his back on the city and headed for Mount Minobu in Yamanashi Prefecture. This was the place where almost three centuries before, Miyamoto Musashi, the greatest Samurai swordsman who had ever lived, trained in isolation to hone his legendary skills.

Yashiro, a close friend and one of Oyama's top Karate students, agreed to go with him to the wilderness. The pair made a pact that they would train on the isolated mountaintop for two years. They sealed the deal by shaving off their hair and eyebrows, a measure to ensure they would face humiliation if they were to return to society too soon.

Oyama and Yashiro built a shack on the side of the mountain and soon began their training. The day would begin with a simple breakfast of rice and vegetables at dawn—their food being dropped off weekly by a friend in a nearby village. The meal was then followed by running and climbing in the forest for hours before punching and kicking trees until their hands and feet were bloody. Finally, they would meditate beneath an ice-cold waterfall until their bodies could take no more. After just a few weeks, the physical and mental pressures from living like hermits and training for twelve hours a day had left Oyama and Yashiro exhausted beyond belief. The grim reality of the situation had set in, and it soon became too much for Yashiro. One night, he waited for his friend and teacher to fall asleep and fled in shame.

For the next three years, Oyama's only human contact was through occasional visits from another friend in a nearby village who would bring him rations and vital supplies. Otherwise, the Karate master remained alone. His only entertainment was Musashi's *Book of Five Rings*, which he read obsessively in order to create his own format of Karate, the likes of which had never been seen before.

Oyama returned to society a changed man, ready to take on the world. The mental and physical strength gained from his time in the wilderness, knowing the depths of despair to which his own mind could plunge, meant he found there was little left to fear from men.

Setting off on a tour of the country, the Karate master journeyed for hundreds of miles, seeking out top fighters to challenge from every renowned school and style across Japan. Hundreds of martial arts experts fell against Oyama; his strikes landed with the force of iron, and his will seemed unbreakable. The Master's conditioning was so intense that many of his opponents broke bones in their arms and legs merely attempting to block his attacks. Most were left in no doubt that his punches or kicks, if delivered without restraint, would kill.

After long contemplation on the name of his new system of Karate, Oyama eventually decided on "Kyokushin," or "Ultimate Truth." His key principle came from the Samurai sword fighting adage: "One strike, certain death." This philosophy was one he knew he must demonstrate for the world to see.

* * *

It had been raining for weeks. Fortunately, the sun had broken through the thick gray clouds that morning and it was becoming a warm spring day when Oyama made his way down towards the waterfront.

He could see a crowd of reporters and spectators that had gathered on the beach, eager to watch what had been dubbed "The Duel of the Century."[2] Oyama took a long, deep breath, trying to keep his focus on the challenge he was about to face.

From across the sand, a group of handlers brought forth his opponent: a one-ton bull with horns four inches thick. The second the infuriated creature was free, it charged. Oyama caught his opponent by the horns and the pair locked into a grappling match. He tried in vain to wrench the bull off balance and pull it down to the sand, but the beast was too strong. When the pair broke free from each other, the bull circled back and charged again. The glaring sunlight made it hard to judge the distance, and the bull caught Oyama in the guts with a horn. Blood gushed from the gaping wound, but despite the pain, he refused to give up. Oyama wrestled the bull for a further thirty minutes before he finally took the exhausted creature to the floor. Holding the animal down, he slammed the outside edge of his hand into the bull's head just below the horn, snapping it clean off with his strike. Finally, the creature's will to fight disappeared. Despite several severe injuries, the Karate master emerged victorious.

Over the course of his career, Oyama survived a further fifty-two public fights with live bulls, three of which he killed with a single strike to the head, earning him the nickname "God-hand."

THE FACTS

Oyama was clearly a great martial artist with incredible strength (a vast number of his students, and video evidence of his feats corroborate this). However, there are several facts about the challenges he faced that are worth further examination.

First, in terms of his early life and the training that Oyama received, nearly all the recorded information comes from his own hand. Possibly because of the sheer quantity of work he produced, the claims within this anthology are sometimes inconsistent and occasionally even contradictory. For example, Oyama states that in Manchuria he "mastered the eighteen techniques of Chinese Kempo."[3] But, owing to the scarcity of records related to this study (such as certifications, photographs, or written records) alongside a lack of references in his later martial arts developments, some argue that his training was likely informal and not extensive.[4]

We can apply this same logic to Oyama's experiences with Judo. Some versions of his life story claim he reached anywhere up to a fourth-degree black belt while at university. However, to achieve such a rank in just four years would be unheard of even today, let alone in post-war Japan.

While it is verifiable that Oyama studied Shotokan under Gichin Funakoshi, his desire to focus on the combative elements of Karate (by turning to Goju-Ryu and So Nei-Chu) is evident from statements in interviews regarding Funakoshi and Shotokan. For example: "It's not Karate. What he (Funakoshi) taught me was etiquette and exercise."

Oyama then describes Funakoshi as "soft and gentle, good for teaching Karate to little children like he did in Okinawa."[5] While the tale of Oyama's "training" in which he would take on American military personnel, also stems from his own writings, it is likely that the surrender and occupation of Japan was traumatic for someone like him, who was "intensely devoted to his country of adoption."[6] Therefore, it is at least plausible that he may have tried to rebel against the American occupants of post-WWII Japan and improve his fighting abilities simultaneously.

Second, referring to his time in the mountains, rather than the common legend of his training being three continuous years, Oyama himself states that he completed two separate stints. The first of these was fourteen months, in which Yashiro *did* abandon him in the night, and he was left to train on his own. The final straw then came when the friend who had arranged to supply him with food wrote saying he could no longer afford to be his sponsor.[7] Oyama claimed he then returned to civilization, fought and won the Karate event in the 1947 Japanese National Martial Arts Championships, and returned to the wilderness for another eighteen months. However, this rendition of events is called into doubt by one of Oyama's top students from the time. Jon Bluming, a Dutch national, was one of the earliest high-ranking foreign Karate practitioners in Japan, and the first to earn a fifth-degree black belt in Kyokushin. He stated that Oyama only trained in the mountains for a number of weeks rather than years.

Bluming also claimed that the alleged championship win in 1947 would have been impossible due to the prohibition of combat sports under American occupation, and that these tales were instead circulated by a foreign co-author in an early edition of one of Oyama's books.[8] While it is well documented that the Karate master did frequently train in the wilderness, kicking and punching trees, smashing rocks, and meditating in icy waterfalls for extended periods of time, the likely conclusion is that the time frame of his mountain training was exaggerated to make his tale more interesting.

Finally, there are various photographs and videos of Oyama taking on bulls, many of which are freely available online. However, the claims that he could regularly smash the horns off bulls with a single blow are unsubstantiated. While there is supposed video footage of him doing so, most edits of such videos cut before he delivers the strike, then display a cleanly broken horn upon the ground.[9] His own students and other participants in these events have also suggested that those he managed to break during bouts had been loosened or cut in advance to prepare for the feat.[10]

Oyama pins a bull to the ground in a 1954 demonstration. It is worth noting that in all photos of the Master performing this feat, the bulls appear to be horned, alive, and relatively uninjured.

FUNCTIONS OF THE LEGEND

Promoting Kyokushin

Mas Oyama was clearly both a natural showman and marketing genius of his day. He wrote dozens of instructional books and spread his style of Karate across the globe by coming up with new challenges and trials to garner public attention. Another example of this is the one-hundred-man Kumite in which Oyama faced a hundred fighters back to back over the course of several days (a feat that even today, only a small number of people have ever managed to complete). However, despite the mysteries surrounding him and his near-extraordinary feats, Oyama's legend offers some practical benefits not only for Kyokushin Karate practitioners, but also martial artists in general.

First, Oyama's legend presents him as a near-superhuman character, which provides "a halo effect"[11] in which association grants practitioners credibility simply by being just a generation or two of masters away from the man himself.

Second, the sheer intensity that Oyama is claimed to have possessed throughout the legend, but also his life, is nothing short of inspirational. His tale is a testament to the philosophy of martial arts that states that there are no limits to what can be achieved through the power of the mind. Whether Oyama met the exact descriptions of the legend or simply lesser versions, they became well-known enough that the master became a living legend.

Providing a Rationale for Physical Practices

Oyama's legend claims that the level of external conditioning he gained from his time training in the wilderness and beyond was so extensive that he could severely injure opponents with a single strike or block. While this may well have been true (intense physical conditioning has long been emphasized in Karate), the legend has also served an important function for modern-day Kyokushin practice.

A crucial component of the style is that full-power strikes are permitted to the torso but no punches or hand attacks are allowed to the face. The reason usually put forth for this is that practitioners (much like the system's founder) are so well conditioned that the strikes are too dangerous while the use of protective gear would be detrimental to the realism of the system.[12] This function, however, is a double-edged sword. While taking repeated blows to the head without protection (or even with it) is dangerous, this could be counteracted by fighting open handed, with reduced force, or by using specially developed equipment. Furthermore, it has been established that automaticity is crucial to the success of self-defense techniques in high-pressure situations.[13] Therefore,

this avoidance of head strikes may ironically be detrimental to the self-defense aspects of the art that Oyama considered so crucial.[14]

Conversely, however, this style of sparring allows continued practice for fighters without sustaining serious facial injuries or requiring a large amount of equipment. In doing so, it offers students a chance to test themselves physically and mentally, somewhat akin to their master. Even though body shots are less likely to cause serious injuries as those to the face, and head kicks are far less easy to land cleanly, taking a well-conditioned punch to the chest is undoubtedly painful!

References & Figures

[1] Adapted from Oyama in Heaney, S. (2017, April 28). "The Early Martial Arts Training of Mas Oyama." The Martial Way. Retrieved October 25, 2021, from http://the-martial-way.com/ the-early-martial-arts-training-of-mas- oyama.

[2] Oyama, M. (1974). *What Is Karate?* Japan Publications. p. 374.

[3] Oyama. (1974). p. 1.

[4] Cowie, R., & Dyson, M. (2016). *A Short History of Karate* (2nd ed.). Kenkyo-ha Goju Karate Kempo Kai.

[5] Adams, A. (1971, October). "The Father of Modern Karate." *Black Belt Magazine.*

[6] Cowie and Dyson. (2016). p. 37.

[7] Oyama. (1974). p. 1.

[8] Mann, W. R. (2008, April 7). "Jon Bluming, Europe's First Mixed Martial Artist." Realfighting Organization. Retrieved October 30, 2021, from https://realfighting.com/jon_bluming.php.

⁹ Mas Oyama's strikes against the bull's horn and convenient cut takes place at 2m 35s. https://www.youtube.com/watch?v=brHuxeV029E.

¹⁰ Smith, R. W. (1999). *Martial Musings: A Portrayal of Martial Arts in the 20th Century.* Via Media Pub. Co.

¹¹ Green, T. A., & Svinth, J. R. (Eds.). (2003). *Martial Arts in the Modern World.* Praeger.

¹² Ekhtiyari, A. (n.d.). *Kyokushin Karate History.* International Karate Organization Kyokushin Sabakido. Retrieved November 25, 2021, from http://www.kyokushin-sabakido.com/kyokushinkai/.

¹³ Angleman, A. J., et al. (2009). "Traditional Martial Arts Versus Modern Self-Defense Training for Women: Some Comments." *Aggression and Violent Behavior* 14(2): 89–93. https://doi.org/10.1016/j.avb.2008.12.001.

¹⁴ "Kyokushin Karate: Is It Effective in a Street Fight and for Self-Defense? Way of Martial Arts." (2020, May 12). Retrieved November 25, 2021, from https://wayofmartialarts.com/kyokushin-karate-is-it-effective-in-a-street-fight-and-for-self-defence/.

The image on page 170 is public domain.

Part V

CONCLUSION

From looking at twelve of the best-known tales of legendary martial artists in relation to their commonly circulated stories, the known facts, and their relevance to modern-day martial artists, there are several key conclusions that we can draw.

First, as briefly discussed in the introduction of this book, there are many similarities between these figures and their tales. Although there is often not a single set type of story that reoccurs, there are definite themes, plot structures, and archetypes that appear to run through them. However, it remains unclear whether these similarities (such as being an underdog who is vastly outnumbered or outweighed, or being a sickly, weak child who is trained by a mysterious old master) are coincidentally absorbed into such stories due to their dramatic appeal or if we simply favor these types of stories. Regardless of this consideration, the legends themselves serve a variety of purposes both historically and through to the modern day. Some key functions include the following:

Establishing Shared Identity Among Practitioners

For example, uniting a particular marginalized or political group. This is especially relevant for modern nation building purposes, such as within post-WWII Korea or Japan, twentieth-century Thailand, and Vietnam. It could be argued that all the countries above have used their martial arts legends to create a shared identity for nationalistic purposes. Meanwhile, creating a shared identity among practitioners takes place all over the world (albeit on a smaller scale) to this very day.

Practitioners often find social acceptance and friendship among groups that they can identify with because of some specific lineage, historical figure, or site. In fact, Donohue states that upon merely donning the uniform of a martial art, the student is offered "a statement of individual conformity and identification with the group."[1]

This may also take the form of providing lineages and orders for certain peoples and practitioners to follow or call their own. For example, the Northern and Southern Shaolin Buddhist orders, Gracie Clan Jiu Jitsu, Bruce Lee's Jeet Kune Do, or even by belonging to a certain genre of martial arts (such as striking, grappling, or weapons).

Providing Legitimization for Physical Practices

Taekwondo, Muay Thai, Kyokushin, Brazilian Jiu Jitsu, Wing Chun, and others have all used the aforementioned legends to provide a rationale for the inclusion of certain techniques, strategies, or even equipment within their training.

Legitimizing physical practices is, however, somewhat of a "chicken or the egg" scenario. Often it is impossible to identify whether the legends have been reworked to include specific techniques, or if the techniques have simply been emphasized due to their roles in the aforementioned legends.

Moral and Spiritual Teachings

Although more apparent in the legends of ancient and mysterious figures such as Bodhidharma, Zhang Sanfeng, Miyamoto Musashi, and Morihei Ueshiba, most of the legends have some kind of overarching lesson that displays moral principles or philosophies. For example, those of Japanese Budo, Taoism, or Buddhism. Although, whether we agree with these lessons or not is a different matter.

Inspiring or Challenging Practitioners

Without a doubt, many of the legends discussed feature extremely impressive acts that are mostly achieved through sheer determination and desire for excellence. Much like the legends told in any sport, these tales serve as inspirations, leading followers to challenge and push themselves further, striving for perfection. This desire for practitioners to one day match the legendary status and skills of their heroes is a powerful thing. Whether martial artists want to prosper in competition and become champions, defend themselves in dangerous scenarios, or even transcend mortality itself, these legends set a high bar to aim for.

Inspiring Societal Change

Whether or not the actual events took place (for example, Bruce Lee being forbidden from teaching his art to non-Chinese, or Gogen Yamaguchi fighting to change the perception of Okinawan martial arts in Japan), they still hold the potential to make large-scale differences. For example, it could be argued that Bruce Lee's tale assisted in bringing the issue of a divide between Chinese and American communities to the forefront of public consciousness, even though it may have been essentially untrue. Similarly, by creating a widespread system of "Ancient Korean" martial arts with Taekwondo, who can deny the physical benefits that having millions of adults with black belts must have provided for South Korea?

Enjoyment

Possibly the most important purpose all of these legends serve in the modern world is that of enjoyment. We all love great stories, and with those that stem from real life (or are at least partially true) our enjoyment is often compounded. While it can be argued that in many cases, we are simply pulling the wool over our own eyes by choosing to believe in "orientalist fantasies,"[2] the fact of the matter is that these legends and stories are fun. As long as the legends we tell do not enable negative behaviors or present negative ramifications to the followers of a martial art, then it is this author's opinion that we should simply be able to enjoy these legends, fact or fiction, for what they are. Whether the tales told about these legendary figures of martial arts are entirely accurate, somewhat accurate, or complete fiction, the purposes they have served historically and continue to serve are real.

Therefore, knowing the facts from the fiction and function should not be detrimental to the way we interact with our chosen disciplines or those of our peers. Instead, we should try to focus on the myriad of benefits, teachings, and enjoyment provided by such stories about the legendary figures of martial arts.

References & Figures

[1] Donohue, J. J. (1993). "The Ritual Dimension of Karate-do." *Journal of Ritual Studies* 7(1): 105–124. http://www.jstor.org/stable/44398891.

[2] Said, E. W. (2019). *Orientalism*. Penguin Books. p. 20.

ABOUT THE AUTHOR

Augustus John Roe is an author and martial artist. Originally from the UK, he has spent the last decade of his life living, training, and writing in Asia.

His home has predominantly been in Vietnam, where he lives with his wife and children. Augustus has trained up to the level of *Võ Sư* (Master) in Vietnamese Kung Fu, as well as training in Taekwondo, Arnis, Wing Chun, Brazilian Jiu Jitsu, Muay Thai, Aikido, Savate, and many other styles.

Augustus is the author of the award-winning book *The Martial Arts of Vietnam—An Overview of History and Styles* as well as fiction works including *Where Tigers Roam—An Epic tale of Adventure in the Far East* and several other novels under the pen name A. J. Roe.

Augustus is always happy to discuss his work or hear comments from readers and welcomes you to contact him via his website or on social media. He also humbly requests that if you enjoyed the book, please leave a review on Amazon, Google, Goodreads, Apple books, or other places—for authors, this small act makes a HUGE difference!

Finally, for more information about any of his work or to sign up for exclusive deals and updates, please visit:

www.AugustusJohnRoe.com
www.AJRoe.com

BOOKS FROM YMAA

101 REFLECTIONS ON TAI CHI CHUAN
108 INSIGHTS INTO TAI CHI CHUAN
A WOMAN'S QIGONG GUIDE
ADVANCING IN TAE KWON DO
ANALYSIS OF GENUINE KARATE
ANALYSIS OF GENUINE KARATE 2
ANALYSIS OF SHAOLIN CHIN NA 2ND ED
ANCIENT CHINESE WEAPONS
ART AND SCIENCE OF STAFF FIGHTING
THE ART AND SCIENCE OF SELF-DEFENSE
ART AND SCIENCE OF STICK FIGHTING
ART OF HOJO UNDO
ARTHRITIS RELIEF, 3D ED.
BACK PAIN RELIEF, 2ND ED.
BAGUAZHANG, 2ND ED.
BRAIN FITNESS
CHIN NA IN GROUND FIGHTING
CHINESE FAST WRESTLING
CHINESE FITNESS
CHINESE TUI NA MASSAGE
COMPLETE MARTIAL ARTIST
COMPREHENSIVE APPLICATIONS OF SHAOLIN CHIN NA
CONFLICT COMMUNICATION
DAO DE JING: A QIGONG INTERPRETATION
DAO IN ACTION
DEFENSIVE TACTICS
DIRTY GROUND
DR. WU'S HEAD MASSAGE
ESSENCE OF SHAOLIN WHITE CRANE
EXPLORING TAI CHI
FACING VIOLENCE
FIGHT LIKE A PHYSICIST
THE FIGHTER'S BODY
FIGHTER'S FACT BOOK 1&2
FIGHTING ARTS
FIGHTING THE PAIN RESISTANT ATTACKER
FIRST DEFENSE
FORCE DECISIONS: A CITIZENS GUIDE
INSIDE TAI CHI
JUDO ADVANTAGE
JUJI GATAME ENCYCLOPEDIA
KARATE SCIENCE
KATA AND THE TRANSMISSION OF KNOWLEDGE
KRAV MAGA COMBATIVES
KRAV MAGA FUNDAMENTAL STRATEGIES
KRAV MAGA PROFESSIONAL TACTICS
KRAV MAGA WEAPON DEFENSES
LITTLE BLACK BOOK OF VIOLENCE
LIUHEBAFA FIVE CHARACTER SECRETS
MARTIAL ARTS OF VIETNAM
MARTIAL ARTS INSTRUCTION
MARTIAL WAY AND ITS VIRTUES
MEDITATIONS ON VIOLENCE
MERIDIAN QIGONG EXERCISES
MINDFUL EXERCISE
MIND INSIDE TAI CHI
MIND INSIDE YANG STYLE TAI CHI CHUAN
NATURAL HEALING WITH QIGONG
NORTHERN SHAOLIN SWORD, 2ND ED.
OKINAWA'S COMPLETE KARATE SYSTEM: ISSHIN RYU
PRINCIPLES OF TRADITIONAL CHINESE MEDICINE
PROTECTOR ETHIC
QIGONG FOR HEALTH & MARTIAL ARTS 2ND ED.
QIGONG FOR TREATING COMMON AILMENTS

QIGONG MASSAGE
QIGONG MEDITATION: EMBRYONIC BREATHING
QIGONG GRAND CIRCULATION
QIGONG MEDITATION: SMALL CIRCULATION
QIGONG, THE SECRET OF YOUTH: DA MO'S CLASSICS
REDEMPTION
ROOT OF CHINESE QIGONG, 2ND ED.
SAMBO ENCYCLOPEDIA
SCALING FORCE
SELF-DEFENSE FOR WOMEN
SHIN GI TAI: KARATE TRAINING
SIMPLE CHINESE MEDICINE
SIMPLE QIGONG EXERCISES FOR HEALTH, 3RD ED.
SIMPLIFIED TAI CHI CHUAN, 2ND ED.
SOLO TRAINING 1&2
SPOTTING DANGER BEFORE IT SPOTS YOU
SPOTTING DANGER BEFORE IT SPOTS YOUR KIDS
SPOTTING DANGER BEFORE IT SPOTS YOUR TEENS
SPOTTING DANGER FOR TRAVELERS
SUMO FOR MIXED MARTIAL ARTS
SUNRISE TAI CHI
SURVIVING ARMED ASSAULTS
TAE KWON DO: THE KOREAN MARTIAL ART
TAEKWONDO BLACK BELT POOMSAE
TAEKWONDO: A PATH TO EXCELLENCE
TAEKWONDO: ANCIENT WISDOM
TAEKWONDO: DEFENSE AGAINST WEAPONS
TAEKWONDO: SPIRIT AND PRACTICE
TAI CHI BALL QIGONG: FOR HEALTH AND MARTIAL ARTS
THE TAI CHI BOOK
TAI CHI CHIN NA, 2ND ED.
TAI CHI CHUAN CLASSICAL YANG STYLE, 2ND ED.
TAI CHI CHUAN MARTIAL POWER, 3RD ED.
TAI CHI CONCEPTS AND EXPERIMENTS
TAI CHI CONNECTIONS
TAI CHI DYNAMICS
TAI CHI FOR DEPRESSION
TAI CHI IN 10 WEEKS
TAI CHI PUSH HANDS
TAI CHI QIGONG, 3RD ED.
TAI CHI SECRETS OF THE ANCIENT MASTERS
TAI CHI SECRETS OF THE WU & LI STYLES
TAI CHI SECRETS OF THE WU STYLE
TAI CHI SECRETS OF THE YANG STYLE
TAI CHI SWORD: CLASSICAL YANG STYLE, 2ND ED.
TAI CHI SWORD FOR BEGINNERS
TAI CHI WALKING
TAI CHI CHUAN THEORY OF DR. YANG, JWING-MING
TRADITIONAL CHINESE HEALTH SECRETS
TRADITIONAL TAEKWONDO
TRAINING FOR SUDDEN VIOLENCE
TRIANGLE HOLD ENCYCLOPEDIA
TRUE WELLNESS SERIES (MIND, HEART, GUT)
WARRIOR'S MANIFESTO
WAY OF KATA
WAY OF SANCHIN KATA
WAY TO BLACK BELT
WESTERN HERBS FOR MARTIAL ARTISTS
WILD GOOSE QIGONG
WING CHUN IN-DEPTH
WINNING FIGHTS
XINGYIQUAN

AND MANY MORE ...

VIDEOS FROM YMAA

more products available from . . .

YMAA Publication Center, Inc. 楊氏東方文化出版中心

1-800-669-8892 • info@ymaa.com • www.ymaa.com

Printed in the USA
CPSIA information can be obtained
at www.ICGtesting.com
JSHW010721130923
48365JS00003B/3